**This book is to be returned on or before
the last date stamped below.**

29. 09. 81

31. OCT 81

19. JAN 82

26. MAY 82

11. JUN 82

30. NOV 82

07. OCT 83

02. JUL 84

17 NOV 1994

44. ...

31. MAR 1997

RENEWALS   *Please quote:* date of return, your ticket number
and computer label number for each item.

WORLD LEADERS IN CONTEXT

CHURCHILL

Madeline Jones

Batsford Academic and
Educational Limited London

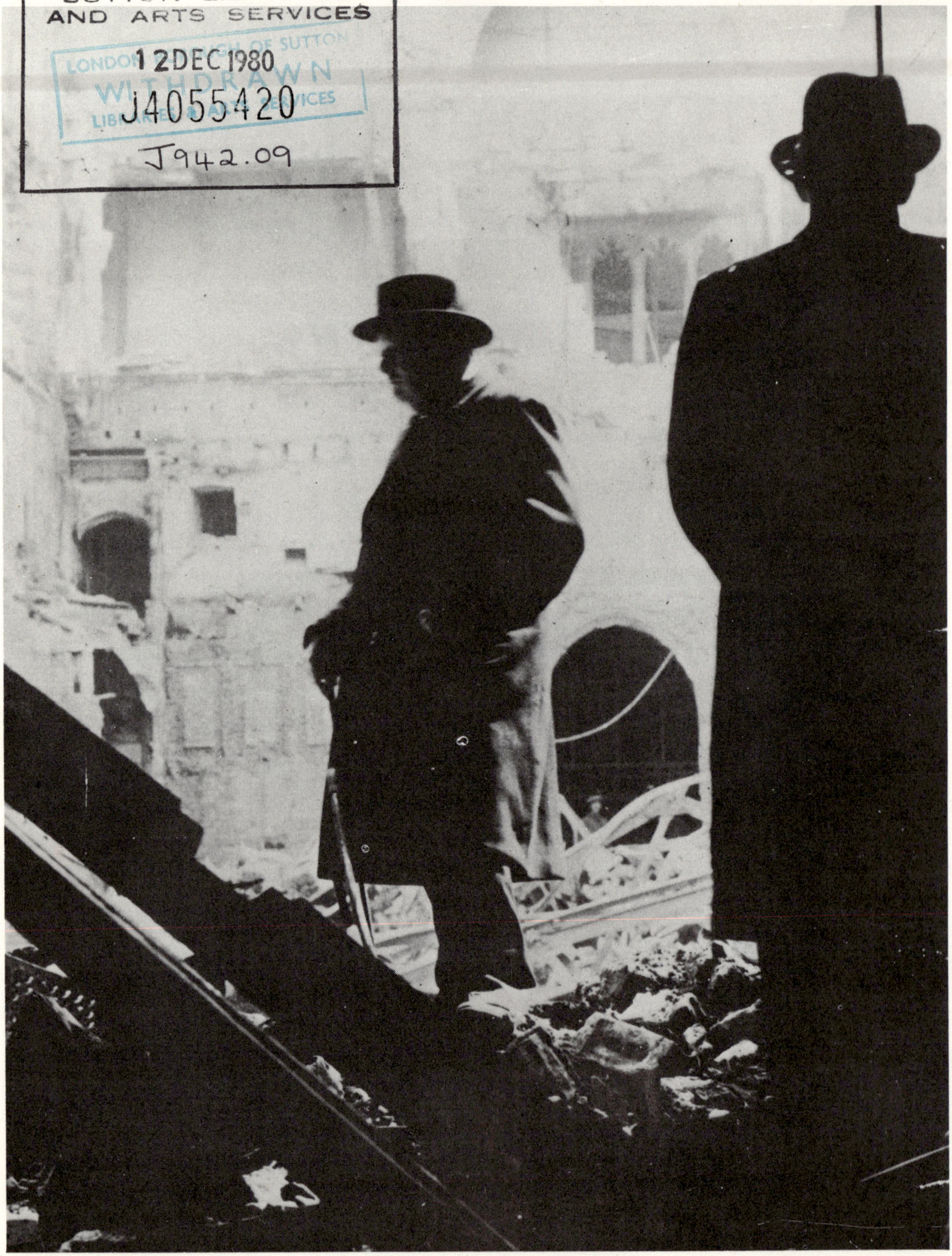

File notes on Winston Churchill

1	FAMILY NAME	CHRISTIAN NAME	MIDDLE NAMES
	Churchill	Winston	Leonard Spencer

2	NATIONALITY
	British

3	PLACE OF BIRTH	4	DATE OF BIRTH
	Blenheim Palace, Oxfordshire		30 November 1874

5	PLACE OF DEATH	6	DATE OF DEATH
	London		24 January 1965

7	FATHER	8	MOTHER
	Lord Randolph Churchill politician born 1849 died 1895		Jennie (née Jerome) nationality American, born 1854 died 1921

9	BROTHERS AND SISTERS
	One brother, John (known as Jack) born 1880 died 1947

10	MARITAL DETAILS
	12 September 1908 married Clementine Hozier died 1977

11	CHILDREN
	Diana, born 1909 died 1963 Randolph, born 1911 died 1968 Sarah, born 1914 Marigold, born 1918 died 1921 Mary, born 1922

12 DESCRIPTION (in late sixties)

HEIGHT	HAIR	EYES	COMPLEXION	PHYSIQUE
5' 8''	reddish, balding	"blue and fierce"	red-faced	fat

13	DISTINGUISHING FEATURES
	Has difficulty in pronouncing letter 's'

14 MAJOR POSTS HELD

Under-Secretary of State for the Colonies, December 1905-April 1908
President of the Board of Trade, April 1908-February 1910
Home Secretary, February 1910-October 1911
First Lord of the Admiralty, October 1911-May 1915
Chancellor of the Duchy of Lancaster, May-November 1915
Minister of Munitions, July 1917-January 1919
Secretary of State for War and Air, January 1919-February 1921
Secretary of State for the Colonies, February 1921-October 1922
Chancellor of the Exchequer, November 1924-June 1929
First Lord of the Admiralty, September 1939-May 1940
Prime Minister and Minister of Defence, May 1940-July 1945
Prime Minister, October 1951-April 1955

First published 1980
© text Madeline Jones 1980
Typeset by Tek-Art Ltd S.E.20
Printed in Hong Kong
for the Publishers Batsford Academic and
Educational Limited,
4 Fitzhardinge Street, London W1H 0AH

ISBN 0 1734 1922 9

Acknowledgment

The Author and Publishers thank the following for
their permission to use the illustrations in this book:
BBC Hulton Picture Library, for figs 1, 2, 5, 6, 7, 9,
10, 12, 13, 15, 17, 19, 20, 25, 27, 31, 47, 49;
Popperfoto, for the frontispiece and figs 3, 4, 8, 11,
14, 16, 18, 22, 23, 24, 26, 28, 29, 30, 32, 33, 34, 35,
36, 37, 38, 39, 40, 41, 42, 43, 44, 45, 46, 48. Alan
Gunston drew the map on page 20. The picture
research was by Peta Hambling.

Thanks are also expressed for the permission to
quote from the following: *Winston S Churchill* by
Randolph Churchill and Martin Gilbert (William
Heinemann Ltd); *History of the Second World War*
by Winston Churchill (Cassell Ltd).

Frontispiece: Churchill surveys the ruins of the
House of Commons, 1941.

Contents

List of Illustrations

Chapter One 1899-1905

The Junior Member for Oldham

An auspicious debut on the platform was made the other day by Mr Winston Churchill, elder son of the late Lord Randolph Churchill. He . . . delighted his audience by the force and mental agility he displayed. Mr Churchill, who is only twenty-three, aspires to a seat in Parliament.

This was how *The Lady* magazine of 5 August 1897 described Churchill's first public speech. He made it at Claverton Manor, near Bath, when he was still an army officer. By the summer of 1899, he was sure that, if he became an MP, he could earn his keep by writing books and newspaper articles (MPs were not paid a salary until 1911). He left the army and stood as Conservative candidate in a by-election at Oldham in Lancashire. On 2 July he wrote to a friend:

> . . . whatever the result may be it has been a strange experience and I shall never forget the succession of great halls packed with excited people until there was not room for one single person more — speech after speech, meeting after meeting — three even four in one night . . . a great experience. And I improve every time . . .

1 In 1895 Churchill was a Lieutenant in the 4th Hussars. He liked army life but was soon thinking of a political career.

Churchill lost, but made a good impression in the town.

South Africa
During the Boer War (1899-1902) Churchill acted as war correspondent in South Africa for the *Morning Post*. He was imprisoned by the Boers in Pretoria in November 1899

TYPHOID AT MAIDSTONE

LORD MAYOR'S OFFER ACCEPTED.

FROM OUR SPECIAL CORRESPONDENT.

MAIDSTONE, Friday Night.

The reply telegraphed by the Mayor of Maidstone to the offer of assistance received yesterday from the Lord Mayor of London, was in the following terms : " Grateful thanks for your Lordship's kind message. Distress must be severe during the coming winter, and funds urgently needed. Assistance in that direction therefore would be most heartily welcomed.—Mayor of Maidstone." In consequence of an announcement in some papers this morning that the authorities of Maidstone did not deem it desirable that a fund should be opened at the Mansion House at present, the Mayor, with the approbation of the Relief Committee, further telegraphed to the Lord Mayor as follows : " The Mayor of Maidstone is much distressed at the statement made in to-day's papers that it is not yet deemed advisable to seek your Lordship's powerful assistance. Such is entirely contrary to the intention of my wire yesterday, and to the earnest wishes of the inhabitants, who, with myself, feel we stand greatly in need of your help."

The relief fund has reached a total of nearly £5,000. Hundreds of letters enclosing subscriptions were received by the Mayor this morning from different parts of the country. Gifts in kind also continue to pour in.

At the present moment the Relief Committee find that the demand for blankets considerably exceeds the supply they have at their disposal,

BIRMINGHAM FESTIVAL

FROM OUR SPECIAL CORRESPONDENT.

BIRMINGHAM, Friday Night.

With an exhausted list of new works, the Festival has spent its closing day in doing honour to some that are old enough to be familiar. The public came to the call of the favourites, and not a place was vacant at either of the performances. Indeed, much money was turned away through want of room for those who offered it as an " Open Sesame." It must be painful for a festival official to refuse cash, so overwhelmingly glad is he to get it ; and, on the other hand, the occasions are rare which call upon him to suffer. Some big figures appear in the returns of the Festival, so far as published. Here are the attendances on the first three days : Tuesday morning (" Elijah "), 1,968 ; Tuesday evening (miscellaneous), 1,302 ; Wednesday morning (Stanford's " Requiem," &c.), 1,185 ; Wednesday evening (" King Arthur," &c.), 1,368 ; Thursday morning (" Messiah "), 1,619 ; Thursday evening (" Ode to the Sea "), 1,266, making a total for the six concerts of 8,708, as against 8,700 in 1894. It will be observed that the " Messiah " and " Elijah " are considerably ahead of any other attraction, their combined audiences numbering 3,587, or considerably more than a third of the whole. The receipts from the sale of tickets and donations were : On Tuesday, £4,528 8s 8d ; on Wednesday, £2,476 3s 4d ; on Thursday, £3,155 18s 10d, making a total of £10,160 10s 10d—an increase upon 1894 of £619 10s. The large audiences of to-day will tell greatly upon the aggregate, and doubtless make a striking advance as compared with the figures of the last Festival. This is highly satisfactory, not only to the funds of the General Hospital, on behalf of which the Festivals are held, but also to lovers of music, which benefits so much from these

THE WAR IN THE INDIAN HIGHLANDS.

By A YOUNG OFFICER.

NAWAGAI, Sept. 12.

In my last letter to you I gave some account of the march of a column of troops in service in India. Since then we have been continuously moving, at a rate varying from eight to fourteen miles a day, and we have now arrived at the entrance of the passes which give access to the country of the Mohmands. The two brigades which compose the force Sir Bindon Blood intends to employ against this tribe move separately under their own brigadiers, but keep within four or five miles of each other, so as to be able to concentrate at the shortest possible notice. Starting by starlight, a halt is made at about eight o'clock for breakfast, and the troops usually reach the camping-ground at midday. Many people have read of the sufferings of the British soldiers in the Indian Mutiny, through being compelled to march and fight in the hot weather. August and September in these parts are as hot as it is agreeable to imagine or elegant to express, and the exposure to the sun is undoubtedly a very severe trial to the European troops. Of course, since 1857 sweeping changes have been made in the dress of the soldier. The pith helmet, with its long covering shade, shields the head and face. A padded spine-protector is buttoned on to the back, and a loose and easy khaki uniform is substituted for the stocks and tunics of former days. But the sun remains the same, and all precautions can only modify without preventing the evil effects. What those effects are, the hospital returns will tell with more force than many words.

The men are so cheery and good-humoured, so

---

2 To earn enough money to go into politics, Churchill wrote articles for newspapers. He is the "young officer" here describing "The War in the Indian Highlands".

and made a daring escape. The Boers put out a description:

> ENGLISHMAN, TWENTY-FIVE YEARS OLD, ABOUT 5FT 8IN HIGH, INDIFF— ERENT BUILD; WALKS A LITTLE WITH A BEND FORWARD; PALE APPEARANCE, RED BROWNISH HAIR; SMALL MOUSTACHE, HARDLY PERCEPTIBLE; TALKS THROUGH THE NOSE; CANNOT PRONOUNCE THE LETTER S PROPERLY; AND DOES NOT KNOW ONE WORD OF DUTCH.

Churchill made his way to Ladysmith where a Captain Gilfillan saw him push through a group of officers, "with a good deal of sang-froid [confidence] and not much ceremony", to talk to the commanding officer General Sir George White — "in a very audible voice".

Gilfillan recorded how

> An older officer said to Sir George, "who on earth is that?" He answered, "That's Randolph Churchill's son Winston; I don't like the fellow, but he'll be Prime Minister of England one day."

Elected to Parliament

Churchill stood again for Oldham in 1900, this time in a general election. He wrote to his mother:

> I am going to have a thorough campaign from the 20th to the 23rd of this month [August], speaking at 2 or 3 meetings every night upon the African question, and trotting through Cotton Mills and Iron works by day . . .

Churchill won a seat by 222 votes, and the Conservative Party won the election.

The first speech Churchill made in Parliament was on "the African question". With

3 The Boers offered a £25 reward for the recapture ▷ of their escaped prisoner.

typical generosity he asked for fair terms to be given to the Boers, once they were defeated. The *Daily Chronicle* of 19 February 1901 reported:

> The rumour had spread through the lobbies that Mr Winston Churchill intended to speak, and, as the clock travelled towards that hour every part of the floor became crowded. The reputation of the father made everyone anxious to see whether the son was his equal, and the achievements of Mr Churchill himself increased the reputation. Mr Churchill is a medium-sized, undistinguished looking young man, with an unfortunate lisp in his voice . . . . All the qualities which made his father the most daring and dauntless of recent Parliamentarians have been missed out in his son . . . . But he has some inherited qualities, candour and independence. The Government must have inwardly rebelled against some of the things he said last night. The speech was in many ways a good one, although it fell short of the father's wonderful skill . . .

Hard work on big speeches

In his autobiography *My Early Life* Churchill wrote:

> In those days, and indeed for many years, I was unable to say anything . . . that I had not written out and committed to memory beforehand.

He worked very hard to make himself a powerful, effective speaker. In 1904 he suffered the most unpleasant experience of drying-up. As *Hansard* tactfully put it:

> The hon. Member . . . faltered in the conclusion of his speech; and, amid sympathetic cheers, resumed his seat, after thanking the House for having listened to him.

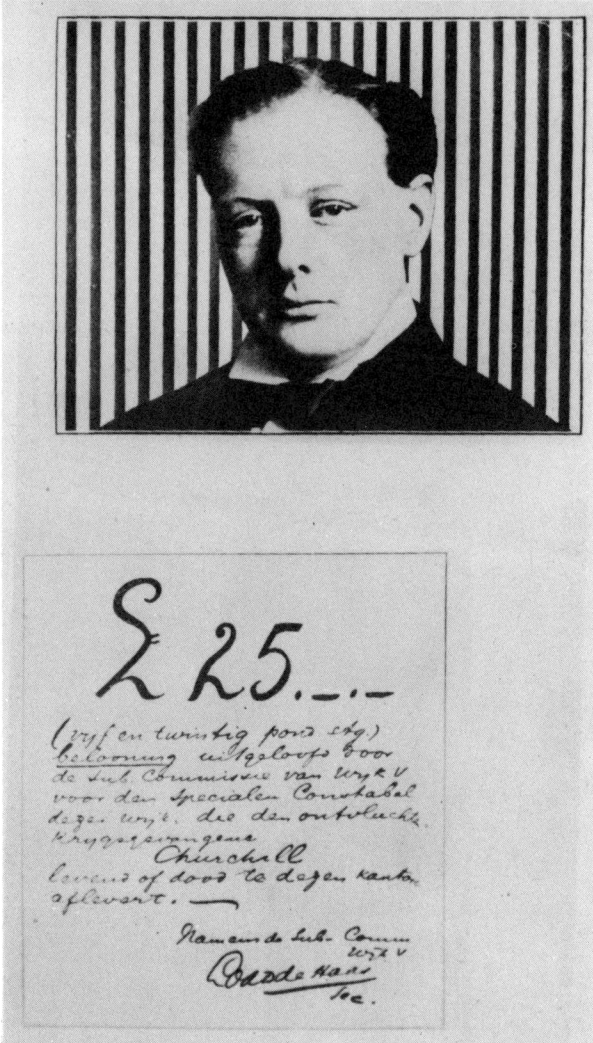

The newspapers were more blunt. The *Daily Mail* announced:

MR CHURCHILL BREAKS DOWN
DRAMATIC SCENE IN THE
HOUSE OF COMMONS

"I suddenly had a complete blackout," Churchill told Lady Violet Bonham-Carter (then Violet Asquith), whose book *Winston Churchill as I knew him* was published in 1965. After the incident, she recorded:

> He continued to learn his speeches by heart but he learnt them (if possible) even more thoroughly than before and armed himself with fuller notes. I have never seen him make a platform speech without a . . . script before him, though he rarely glanced at it.

Making enemies

Churchill's speeches often challenged the policies of his own party and this shocked some Conservatives. His speech (as a very new, very young MP) on 13 May 1901, attacking a Conservative minister's high spending on the army, was typical:

> I cannot follow my right hon. friend on this occasion as I have followed him in the past, and as I hope to follow him in the future. I wish to complain very respectfully, but most urgently, that the Army Estimates . . . are much too high and ought to be reduced . . .

Senior Conservatives grew worried, as the following letter from Joseph Chamberlain to Churchill shows:

> 15 August 1903
> I have felt for a long time . . . that you would never settle down in the position of what is called a "loyal supporter" . . . .
>   P.S. Is it really necessary to be quite

4   Churchill was one of the two MPs for Oldham, an industrial town in Lancashire, from 1900 to 1906.

> as personal in your speeches? You can attack a policy without imputing all sorts of crimes to its authors.

Even his friends found him a trial: Lord Hugh Cecil wrote to him in December 1903:

> What is the use of settling elaborately with you what is to be done if at once you go and do just the opposite . . . .
>   It is not only the folly . . . that fills me with despair. It is your lamentable instability . . . . This instability makes you quite impossible to work with; and will unless you can cure it be a fatal danger to your career.

Another contemporary later commented:

> . . . In the 1900 Parliament Churchill made no attempt to dispel the suspicion and dislike with which he was regarded

by the majority of the House of Commons. He seemed to enjoy causing resentment.

The break with the Conservatives

By the end of 1903 Churchill disagreed with the Conservatives over many matters, and especially over Joseph Chamberlain's plans for Tariff Reform (high customs duties on foreign imports). He himself believed passionately in Free Trade. In December 1903 the Oldham Conservatives told him they did not want him as their candidate in the next election. In the House of Commons he moved into a seat away from the Conservative MPs. The *Times* of 9 April 1904 reported:

> Mr Churchill has we understand been approached by the Liberals of North West Manchester with a view to his becoming

5 In 1906 the ambitious young MP became a junior Minister in the new Liberal government.

their candidate . . . at the next election . . .

The 1906 Election

In January 1906 Churchill fought his new North West Manchester constituency as a Liberal. The *Daily Mail* headlines read:

"WINSTON"
MORE INTERESTING THAN FREE TRADE
HIS JU-JITSU
HE SETS A FASHION IN HATS

His Conservative rival tried to embarrass him by producing a pamphlet with all the past remarks Churchill had made about the Liberal Party — but the new Liberal calmly replied:

> I said a lot of stupid things when I worked with the Conservative Party, and I left it because I did not want to go on saying stupid things.

The Liberals won the election.

Chapter Two 1906-1911

The Liberal Minister

Appointed Under-Secretary for the Colonies by the new Liberal government in 1905, Churchill was now a junior Minister and had to learn to get on with his colleagues. His chief, Lord Elgin, the Secretary of State for the Colonies, later wrote: "When I accepted Churchill as my Under Secretary, I knew I should have no easy task". Churchill poured out ideas and suggestions. He once ended a long paper with the words "These are my views". "But not mine", added Lord Elgin. Even so, at the end of their first year together Churchill wrote:

No one could ever have had a more trustful and indulgent chief . . . . I have learned a very great deal . . . from your instruction and example . . .

Opinions of Churchill

Civil servants at the Colonial Office found Churchill arrogant. When Churchill visited East Africa in 1907, the governor of Uganda complained that he was "a perfect nuisance, dodging about with his camera all the time". Conservatives hated him as a turncoat. When he lost his seat in Parliament at a by-election in 1908, the Conservative *Daily Telegraph* reported:

Churchill out — language fails us just when it is most needed. We have all been yearning for this to happen — Winston

Churchill is out, OUT, OUT!

A few weeks later Churchill won another by-election at Dundee and returned to Parliament.

Social reform

In a speech of 1906 Churchill said:

the State must increasingly and earnestly concern itself with the care of the sick and the aged, and, above all, of the children.

He had become interested in contemporary proposals for improving the life of the poor. He even took books on Socialism with him to East Africa. "They are going to be my reading on the voyage", he told a friend. "I'm going to see what the Socialist case really is".

Although he was never convinced by "the Socialist case", he wholeheartedly supported Liberal reforms. As President of the Board of Trade from 1908, he set up labour exchanges to help the unemployed find work. He spoke too in favour of an eight-hour day for miners, and in 1909 supported Lloyd George's People's Budget against the

6 Although he was interested in reforms which ▷ would help the poor, Churchill's own life was that of a wealthy aristocrat. Here he watches a sports display at Blenheim Palace, home of his cousin the Duke of Marlborough. Typically he stands on a chair to get a really good view.

House of Lords. At the same time, he saw that it could add to his own reputation if he could be seen to be responsible for major reforms. He wrote to his wife in 1911 about the government's plans for a scheme of National Insurance:

> Lloyd George has practically taken Unemployment Insurance to his own bosom, and I am I think effectively elbowed out of this large field in which I consumed so much thought and effort. Never mind! There are many good fish in the sea.

Churchill did not always seem a convincing champion of social reform. The Liberal Charles Masterman commented in 1908:

> He [Winston] is full of the poor whom he has just discovered. He thinks he is called by providence to do something for them.

Lady Violet Bonham-Carter explains in her book why Churchill seemed even to his friends to be out of touch with the poor and their problems:

> Though he had supported himself by his own tireless industry he was not acquainted with poverty. As he once said to me, 'I have always had to earn every penny I possessed, but there has never been a day in my life when I could not order a bottle of champagne for myself and offer another to a friend.' . . . I doubt if he had ever packed his own clothes. It was far simpler to ring a bell — and throughout his life the bells he rang were always answered.

Home Secretary

In 1910 Churchill became Home Secretary, responsible for law and order. He was responsible for prisons too, and remembered from his experience in the Boer War what it was like to be a prisoner:

> They must have food for thought — plenty of books — that's what I missed most — except of course the chance of breaking bounds and getting out of the damned place — and I suppose I mustn't give them *that*!

He did give prisoners lectures and concerts,

7 Sidney Street, January 1911. The gunmen were in the house marked with a cross.

and he cut down the use of solitary confinement. A part of his work that he detested was deciding whether prisoners sentenced to death should or should not be executed.

The "Sidney Street Affair"

Churchill's critics had always accused him of showing-off, and friends like Lloyd George agreed that "he likes the limelight". In 1911 Churchill confirmed this view by rushing straight off to Stepney when he heard that a group of armed men, possibly anarchists, were penned up in a house there in Sidney Street. He wrote to the Prime Minister, Asquith, on 3 January 1911:

> I was interrupted in copying out this letter by the Stepney affair from which I have just returned. It was a striking scene in a London street — firing from every window, bullets chipping the brickwork, police and Scots Guards armed with loaded weapons, artillery jingling up etc. I thought it better to let the house burn down rather than spend good British lives in rescuing these ferocious rascals.

The Conservative ex-Prime Minister, Balfour, commented in Parliament:

> We are concerned to observe photographs in the illustrated papers of the Home

Secretary in the danger zone. I understand what the photographer was doing, but what was the right honourable gentleman doing?

Churchill himself later admitted: "I should have done much better to have remained quietly in my office". What he said at the time, when asked by Charles Masterman "What the hell have you been doing now, Winston?", was "Now, Charlie. Don't be cross. It was such fun."

Industrial unrest

Churchill was accused of over-reacting to a wave of strikes in 1910 and 1911. At Tonypandy (a town in the Rhondda valley, South Wales) in November 1910 there were riots, and soldiers were sent to the area. Churchill reported to King George V:

> No need for the employment of the military is likely to occur. They will be kept as far as possible out of touch with the population, while sufficiently near to the scene to be available if necessary.

However, 300 London policemen were ordered to help the local Welsh Police. Demands were made later in the House of Commons for an inquiry into allegations of police brutality. The MP for the Rhondda, Mr Abraham, said:

> If he [Churchill] wants to clear the character of the men of the Rhondda

and of the police, as I believe he does, there is but one way to do it, and that is to grant this inquiry to see who really caused the disturbances.

The Labour MP Keir Hardie, who sat for a Welsh constituency, had bitterly attacked Churchill in speeches up and down the country. He now gave examples of complaints against the police. Churchill refused an inquiry, and pointed out that Conservatives had also attacked him, "not for the excessive amount of force employed, but for not employing sufficient force". He stressed that, in his view:

> For soldiers to fire on the people would be a catastrophe in our national life.

The Railway Strike, 1911

Unhappily, this very "catastrophe" occurred in the summer of 1911, during a big railway strike which greatly alarmed the government. Early in the dispute Churchill told the King:

> The difficulty is not to maintain order but to maintain order without loss of life.

He also pointed out that the workers' discontent was "due mainly to the fact that wages have not in late years kept pace with the increased cost of living". However, he was ready to use more troops this time than at Tonypandy and to use them less discreetly. Two men were shot by soldiers at Llanelly and Keir Hardie produced a pamphlet called *Killing No Murder* in which he wrote:

> As showing how the troops were likely to be used to shoot men down like dogs, take what happened at Llanelly. A train was stopped by a crowd of strikers squatting down on the line in front of it. Some troops . . . rushed up at the double . . . . But for the presence of the soldiers nothing more would have happened. Some boys and youths did pelt stones at the soldiers, and one of them was struck . . . the officer in command ordered the people to disperse; he gave them one minute in which to do so; at the end of the minute he ordered five shots to be fired which killed two men outright . . . . John Johns, one of the murdered men, was sitting on the garden wall of his own house . . . looking on; the other was also in his garden. No one has ever alleged that either of them threw stones . . .

The events at Llanelly combined with memories of Tonypandy to make the "myth of Tonypandy" — the false belief that Churchill had sent soldiers into action against Tonypandy miners. This, rather than his work for the 1911 Mines Act which improved safety in the pits, stuck in people's minds. Working people mistrusted him from this time on. Even in May 1979 a newspaper reporter for the *Guardian*, talking to an 87 year-old ex-docker about Churchill, was told:

> He might have been a hero, but he was no friend of the working class".

◁ 8   One of the "photographs in the illustrated papers of the Home Secretary in the danger zone" at Sidney Street.

Chapter Three 1911-1915
At the Admiralty

In September 1911 Churchill was staying with the Asquiths in Scotland. One afternoon he took Violet Asquith for a walk to tell her:

> I don't want tea — I don't want anything — anything in the world. Your father has just offered me the Admiralty.

He was officially appointed First Lord of the Admiralty (the title given to the minister in charge of the Navy) in October 1911.

Churchill threw himself into his new work:

> Saturdays, Sundays and every spare day were spent with the Fleets at Portsmouth, Portland, Devonport or visiting dockyards and shipyards throughout the British Isles and Mediterranean.

Even when Churchill took friends for a holiday cruise on the Admiralty yacht, the *Enchantress*, his mind was on his work: Violet Bonham-Carter wrote in *Winston Churchill as I knew him:*

> As we leaned side by side . . . gliding past the lovely, smiling coast-line of the Adriatic, bathed in sun, and I remarked 'How perfect', he startled me by his reply: 'Yes — range perfect — visibility perfect — if we had got some six-inch guns on board how easily we could bombard . . . ' etc. etc — and details followed showing how effectively we could lay waste the landscape

and blow the nestling towns sky-high . . .

It seemed to some people that the new First Lord was all too interested in warfare. A Labour MP, Ramsay MacDonald, wrote in a newspaper article in 1913:

> Mr Churchill is a very dangerous person to put at the head of either of our fighting services. He treats them as hobbies.

Yet Churchill was well aware of the suffering that war brought. As a young army officer in 1899 he had written:

> war, disguise it as you may, is but a dirty, shoddy business, which only a fool would undertake.

Fighting for the Navy

In the Cabinet Churchill argued with his colleagues to get money for the expansion of the Navy. The Chancellor of the Duchy of Lancaster, Charles Hobhouse, kept a diary. His unflattering comments show how irritating Churchill could be.

> 17 July 1912 At Cabinet
> Churchill was most abusive and insulting . . . . He is really a spoilt child endowed by some chance with the brain of a genius.
>
> 13 August 1912
> Churchill is ill mannered, boastful, unprincipled, without any redeeming qualities except his amazing ability and industry.

27 November 1912
We had the usual display of bad manners and bad temper from Churchill. He proposed a fortnight ago an increase of £500,000 for Navy pay. The Estimates Committee cut this down to £300,000. At this he stormed, sulked, interrupted. Like an ill-bred cub.

Churchill annoyed others as well as Hobhouse. Asquith wrote in January 1914:

it is curious what personal hostility Winston excites even in the most unexpected quarters.

Part of the trouble was that in 1909 Churchill had been eager to cut spending on the Navy. Did he now, people asked, want to build more battleships just because the Navy was *his* special concern? Churchill argued that things had changed since, in 1912, the German Emperor had announced an increase in German sea-power. In a speech in Glasgow he pointed out:

9 The young, active First Lord spent "every spare day" with the Fleet.

The British Navy is to us a necessity and from some points of view the German Navy is to them more in the nature of a luxury. Our naval power involves British existence. It is existence for us, it is expansion to them.

Ireland

Churchill provoked more hostility by his attitude to Ireland and the problems of Irish Home Rule. In 1914 he reacted strongly to threats of rebellion by Ulster Protestants who resisted Home Rule. Speaking at Bradford on 14 March he said:

This is the issue — whether civil and Parliamentary government in these realms is to be beaten down by the menace of armed force . . .

He ordered ships of the Royal Navy to take part in a "practice" near the Irish coast, and said that "if Belfast showed fight his fleet

10 The first Dreadnought battleship. The British Navy was determined to have more of these powerful modern ships than the Germans had.

would have the town in ruins in twenty-four hours". Behind the scenes, he worked for a compromise, but the Conservatives bitterly resented his provocative speeches and actions.

War with Germany

Churchill did not at first fear Germany as a rival to Great Britain. In 1908 he said:

Although there may be snapping and snarling in the newspapers and in the London Press, these two great peoples have nothing to fight about, have no prize to fight for and have no place to fight in.

However, from 1912 onwards he became alarmed and, as we have seen, he took care to strengthen the British Navy. Once the crisis of July 1914 developed, he prepared for battle — with relish, some thought. Asquith said:

Winston who has a pictorial mind brimming with ideas is in tearing spirits at the prospect of war, which to me shows lack of imagination.

Churchill very fairly summed up his own mixed attitude in a letter to his wife:

Everything tends towards catastrophe and collapse. I am interested, geared up and happy. Is it not horrible to be built like that? The preparations have a hideous fascination for me . . . . Yet I would do my best for peace, and nothing would induce me wrongfully to strike the blow.

Together with Prince Louis of Battenberg, the First Sea Lord, he saw that the British ships were kept together after their summer exercises, and then secretly sailed round from the English Channel to their war station at Scapa Flow in Scotland. For years to come, Churchill was proud that, when war was declared on 4 August, "The fleet was ready".

Antwerp

Churchill was keenly interested in military

11 A cartoon of 1914, called "And He Gets It: Oliver Twist (a new version)". It shows Churchill successfully demanding more money to spend on the Navy.

as well as naval affairs — and, his critics thought, much too ready to interfere. In October 1914 Asquith heard from Churchill who was in Antwerp, helping to stiffen Belgian resistance against a German attack. Asquith sent Churchill's telegram to a friend, remarking:

> I found when I arrived here this morning the enclosed telegram from Winston, who as you will see, proposed to resign his office (i.e. the Admiralty) in order to take the command in the field . . . W is an ex-Lieutenant . . . and would if his proposal had been accepted, have been in command of 2 distinguished Major-Generals, not to mention Brigadiers, Colonels etc.

Churchill had got carried away by enthusiasm, and was tactfully told by the Prime Minister that he could not be spared. His efforts failed to prevent the capture of Antwerp, although they probably delayed it.

Two reports reflect attitudes to Churchill's presence in Belgium at this time. An Italian war correspondent was impressed when he visited the front:

12 Churchill discussing business with Admiral Fisher. Although Churchill insisted on Fisher's appointment as First Sea Lord, the two men soon found it impossible to agree. Notice the map of the Dardanelles on the wall.

> . . . in the midst of a group of officers stood a man. He was still young, and was enveloped in a cloak, and on his head wore a yachtman's cap. He was tranquilly smoking a large cigar and looking at the progress of the battle under a rain of shrapnel . . . . It was Mr Churchill, who had come to view the situation himself. It must be confessed that it is not easy to find in the whole of Europe a Minister who would be capable of smoking peacefully under that shellfire . . .

Ableseaman Jack Bentham, a young man in one of the Naval Brigades, which had been ordered to Belgium without proper training or equipment, reacted very differently. He wrote to his father:

> We cursed a car containing Churchill who came out to see what was going on and we were glad when he departed . . .

A controversial appointment

When Prince Louis of Battenberg had to resign, following a press campaign against him because of his German blood, Churchill decided that he needed a determined, energetic First Sea Lord. He chose Admiral Fisher, an old friend, now retired. Fisher had a difficult personality, and both Asquith and King George V were worried about appointing him. Asquith wrote in October 1914:

> After lunch I went to see the King, on Winston's business . . . . He gave me an exhaustive and really eloquent catalogue of the old man's [Fisher's] crimes and defects, and thought that his appointment would be very badly received by the bulk of the Navy, and that he would be almost certain to get on badly with Winston . . . . I hope his apprehensions won't turn out to be well founded.

Strategy

By the winter of 1914 the fighting in Western Europe had bogged down, with neither side able to advance. A long period of trench warfare had begun. Churchill realized this, and hated the heavy casualties that the occasional battles brought. He wrote to Asquith:

> I think it quite possible that neither side will have the strength to penetrate the

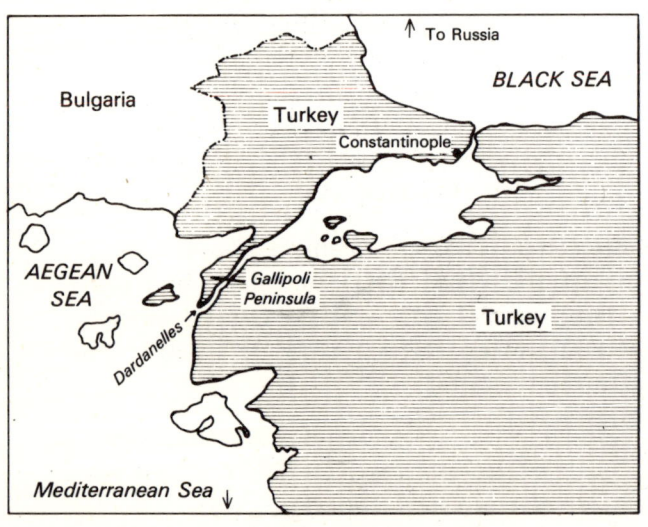

other's lines . . . my impression is that the position of both armies is not likely to undergo any decisive change — although no doubt several hundred thousand men will be spent to satisfy the military mind on the point . . . . Are there not other alternatives than sending our armies to chew barbed wire in Flanders? Further, cannot the power of the Navy be brought . . . to bear upon the enemy?

The Dardanelles

Churchill formed a plan for the Navy to seize the Dardanelles from Germany's ally, Turkey, and on 13 January 1915 he won the support of the War Council for this plan. Maurice Hankey, Secretary to the Committee of Imperial Defence, later recorded:

> The idea caught on at once. The whole atmosphere changed. Fatigue was forgotten. The War Council turned eagerly from the dreary vista of a 'slogging match' on the Western Front to brighter prospects, as they seemed, in the Mediterranean . . . . Churchill unfolded his plans with the skill that might be expected of him, lucidly but quietly and without exaggerated optimism.

Some of the Naval advisers at the Admiralty were doubtful, but Churchill persuaded them. He also persuaded Fisher not to oppose the plan.

The attack on the Dardanelles, which was staged in March 1915, and an attempt to capture the Gallipoli peninsula in April both failed. Most people blamed Churchill. They said he had underestimated the difficulties. Admiral Wilson later recalled:

> [Churchill] kept on saying that he could do it without the army; he only wanted the army to come in and reap the fruits, I think, was his expression; and I think he generally minimised the risks from mobile guns . . .

Churchill pressed for more and more reinforcements for the Dardanelles campaign.

Fisher wrote in his resignation letter on 15 May 1915:

> . . . I find it increasingly difficult to adjust myself to the increasingly daily requirements of the Dardanelles to meet your views — as you truly said yesterday I am in the position of continually vetoing your proposals . . .

The *Times* accused Churchill in an editorial on 18 May 1915 of

> assuming responsibilities and over-riding his expert advisers to a degree which might at any time endanger the national safety.

Churchill summed up his own views in July 1915:

> We have always sent two-thirds of what was necessary a month too late.

13 Hard fighting by British and Dominion troops failed to capture the Gallipoli peninsula in 1915.

He was sure that if the Navy had tried again after the failure of its original attack on 18 March, the British could have seized the Dardanelles:

> The battle . . . could have been resumed a month later in overwhelmingly favourable conditions; and had it been resumed it would, in a few hours, have become apparent that it could have only one ending.

He may have been right.

Removal from office

Fisher's resignation as First Sea Lord in May 1915 and his protests over the Dardanelles campaign gave Churchill's enemies an excuse to attack him. Asquith now wanted a coalition with the Conservatives, and they would not join the government until Churchill was removed from the Admiralty. He fought hard to stay, writing to Asquith on 21 May that his removal

> might lead to the abandonment of the whole Dardanelles operation — which otherwise is a certainty, and then on my head for all time would be the blood of 30,000 brave men who have fallen, killed or wounded or sunk in deep water . . .
> It is no clinging to office or to this particular office or my own interest or advancement which moves me. I am clinging to my *task* and to my *duty* . . .

Asquith replied:

> My dear Winston,
>   I have your letters. You must take it as settled that you are not to remain at the Admiralty . . .

Mrs Churchill felt that the Prime Minister had failed to stand by her husband. She too wrote to him:

> Winston may in your eyes and in those with whom he has to work have faults but he has the supreme quality which I venture to say very few of your present or future Cabinet possess, the power, the imagination, the deadliness to fight Germany.

Many years later she told Churchill's biographer, Martin Gilbert:

> The Dardanelles haunted him for the rest of his life. He always believed in it. When he left the Admiralty he thought he was finished . . .
> I thought he would never get over the Dardanelles; I thought he would die of grief.

Often in the future, Churchill's speeches at election meetings, and even in the House of Commons, were interrupted with shouts of "What about the Dardanelles?"

Chapter Four 1915-1922

Coalition

Churchill held a minor government post for a few months in 1915 after leaving the Admiralty. Then in November he resigned, to go to fight in France. Max Aitken (later Lord Beaverbrook) visited him just before he left:

> The whole household was upside down while the soldier-statesman was buckling on his sword. Downstairs, Mr Eddie Marsh, his faithful secretary, was in tears . . . . Upstairs, Lady Randolph was in a state of despair at the idea of her brilliant son being relegated to the trenches. Mrs Churchill seemed to be the only person who remained calm, collected and efficient.

Colonel Churchill

When Churchill was given command of the 6th Royal Scots Fusiliers in December 1915, he had to convince the officers and men that he was more than just a visiting politician. When the news spread of his appointment, wrote Captain Gibb,

> a mutinous spirit grew . . . any position at all in the Expeditionary Force seemed not too exalted for Winston if only he had left us our own C.O. [commanding-officer] and refrained from disturbing the peace.

14 "Colonel Churchill" in France 1916.

15 Churchill as Minister of Munitions speaking to workers (including many women) in the North of England in 1918.

However, Churchill proved to be a brave and efficient commander, and Captain Gibb wrote of his farewell to his officers in May 1916:

> I believe every man in the room felt Winston Churchill's leaving us a real personal loss.

Churchill left the army in May 1916, in order to return to politics. He felt he had learnt a great deal from serving in the trenches. In February 1916 he had written to his wife:

> . . . there is great lack of 'drive' through-out the administration of the army . . . . This war is one of mechanics and brains and mere sacrifice of brave and devoted

infantry is no substitute and never will be. By God I would make them skip if I had the power — even for a month.

A bad reputation in politics

In March 1916 Churchill, while on leave, had attacked government naval policies in Parliament. He astonished everyone by ending his speech with a sudden appeal for the re-appointment of Fisher as First Sea Lord. Churchill felt that Fisher would get things done — and he was himself always ready to forget a quarrel. Others could not forget so easily. As Admiral Sir Hedworth Meux pointed out:

> The hon and gallant Member [Churchill] is a very old friend of mine, and I have received many kindnesses from him, but there are limits to endurance. When the late First Lord (Colonel Churchill) and Lord Fisher were at the Admiralty they

16 ''Winston's Bag'' (1920). The cartoonist Low here reminds the public of Churchill's past misadventures. The caption reads 'He Hunts Lions and Brings Home Decayed Cats.'

were at daggers drawn, and everybody at the Admiralty knew it. Are we to have all that over again? . . . We all wish him a great deal of success in France, and we hope that he will stay there.

It took Churchill a long time to live down his reputation for wild ideas. He was not given another government post until July 1917, when Lloyd George, the new Prime Minister, made him Minister of Munitions. The Conservative newspaper, the *Morning Post*, commented:

We confidently anticipate that he will continue to make colossal blunders at the cost of the nation.

Back in office

Churchill worked hard to produce munitions, and he had learnt to be a little more cautious. Sir Maurice Hankey saw him on 22 July 1917:

On the whole he was in a chastened mood. He admitted to me that he had been 'a bit above himself' at the Admiralty, and surprised me by saying that he had no idea of the depth of public opinion against his return to public life, until his appointment was made.

However, Churchill could still not resist giving other people advice. The Commander-in-Chief in France, Haig, wrote:

I have no doubt that Winston means to do his utmost to provide the Army with all it requires, but at the same time he can hardly help meddling in the larger questions of strategy and tactics; for the solution of the latter he has had no real training, and his agile mind only makes him a danger.

Churchill's ''agile mind'' helped him to see the advantages of modern weapons. He urged on the development of tanks and machine-guns, as well as aeroplanes.

The end of the Great War

On 11 November 1918 the war ended. Churchill was always generous in victory and even before the fighting ended he stressed that

We are not asking for the unconditional surrender of the German nation . . . . We do not seek to ruin Germany.

Intervention in Russia

After the end of the German war, British troops continued to fight in Russia. They were helping the White Russians, who supported the old Russian government, against the Bolsheviks, who had seized power in the revolution of October 1917. Churchill was made Secretary for War in January 1919 and he strongly favoured the British ''intervention'' in Russian affairs. He was sure that the Bolsheviks

represented a mere fraction of the population, and would be exposed and swept

17   A group of "Black and Tans" in 1921.

away by a General Election.

He hated the bloodshed of revolution and feared the spread of Bolshevik ideas. The War Cabinet minutes for 17 March 1919 record:

> Mr Churchill . . . said the War Cabinet must face the fact that the North of Russia would be over-run by the Bolsheviks, and many people would be murdered. It was idle to think we should escape by sitting still and doing nothing. Bolshevism was not sitting still. It was advancing . . .

Lloyd George, who soon realized that the Russians would unite against foreign interference, eventually supported the withdrawal of British troops — leaving the White Russians, as Churchill pointed out, "to be at the mercy of the Bolsheviks". Again

Churchill, who had not started the policy of intervention although he certainly supported it, got most of the blame. Sir Henry Wilson, Chief of the Imperial General Staff, commented in March 1920:

> So ends in practical disaster another of Winston's military attempts — Antwerp, Dardanelles, Denikin [Denikin was one of the White Russian leaders].

Ireland

Churchill, as Secretary for War, had to take action in Ireland, where the South wanted independence but most people in the North (Ulster) did not. He had told Lloyd George in 1918:

> I have always shared your view that Home Rule should be given to that part which so earnestly desires it and cannot be forced upon that part [i.e. Ulster] which at present distrusts it.

26

In 1919 when the IRA, who wanted the whole of Ireland to become independent, began to use force, Churchill reacted as strongly as he had done against the Ulster rebels in 1914. He told the Cabinet in November 1920:

> It is for consideration whether a policy of reprisals . . . would not be right at the present time.

He raised a special force, the "Black and Tans", to go to Ireland, where they gained a bad reputation for brutality. However, as Colonial Secretary after February 1921, he worked for peace in Ireland. In May 1921 he urged other members of the Cabinet to support a truce:

> It is of great public importance to get a respite in Ireland. I don't agree that it would be a sign of weakness. It would be six or eight months ago. Then we were not in a position to make any concessions and we had to stand firm and we did so. Now our forces are stronger . . . . If you are strong enough you should make the effort . . .

Michael Collins, one of the Irish leaders, was not at first impressed by Churchill, writing of him:

> will sacrifice all for political gain . . . thinks about his constituents, effect of so and so on them. Inclined to be bombastic. Full of ex-officer jingo or similar outlook. Don't actually trust him.

Later, when there was civil war in Ireland and Collins was killed defending the settlement made with Britain by the Irish Treaty of December 1921, he remembered Churchill's support. His last message was:

> Tell Winston we could never have done without him.

18 Churchill relaxing at the French resort of Deauville in 1922.

Opinions of Churchill

Churchill won respect for what George V described as the "skill, patience and tact" he used in Ireland. He was also thought to have done as well as anyone could with Arab and Jewish problems in Palestine. The Conservatives liked his anti-Bolshevik stand, though not much else about him. He was still a difficult colleague, as a letter from Lord Curzon, the Foreign Secretary, shows:

> 9 November 1921
> My dear Winston,
>   I find it very difficult to conduct foreign affairs at all under the conditions which are constantly created, not infrequently by yourself at Cabinet meetings . . . . I often wonder what would be your attitude if in the administration of your department you were subject to the constant interference of a colleague from which I have to

suffer. Indeed I know — for I well recollect
. . . when you would not brook the
slightest criticism of a policy for which
you said you were responsible . . .

Churchill as usual could not see why people
objected to receiving his advice:

> 9 November 1921
> My dear George,
>   . . . Ever since I entered the Cabinet
> in 1908, it has always been customary
> for questions of foreign affairs to be freely
> discussed . . . . There is absolutely no
> comparison between issues in Foreign
> affairs and those which arise in ordinary
> departments . . . . I never knew Sir Edward
> Grey [Asquith's Foreign Secretary] to
> complain . . .

Drift to the Conservatives

Entries in the diary of Tom Jones, the Assist-
ant Secretary to the Cabinet, for June 1922,
when Churchill was much occupied with
Ireland, reflect his increasingly stormy relationship with Lloyd George:

> 7 June 1922
> He [Churchill] said if the P.M. [Lloyd
> George] were going to butt in he could
> take the business on himself and have his
> resignation.

> 8 June 1922
> . . . there was a good deal of talk about
> Churchill's disloyalty as a colleague. 'No
> Churchill was ever loyal' remarked the
> P.M. 'Churchill is fancying himself as a
> leader of a Tory revolt' . . . the P.M.
> compared Winston to a chauffeur who
> apparently is perfectly sane and drives
> with great skill for months, then suddenly

he takes you over a precipice . . .

Churchill was indeed starting to feel that he
had more in common with the Conservatives
than with the Liberals now.

The Chanak crisis

However, Churchill agreed with Lloyd George
that it was necessary to stand up to a threat
by the Turks against British troops based
at Chanak. The Cabinet minutes for 29
September 1922 record that Churchill

> himself . . . did not take a tragic view of the
> situation and had by no means lost hope
> that there might still be a peaceful settle-
> ment . . . . He could hardly believe that
> Mustapha Kemal [the Turkish leader]
> wished to embroil himself with us. What
> Mustapha Kemal thought and what had
> been dinned into him was that the British
> could be trampled on and ignored. He
> might get over that idea if a lesson were
> given him locally at Chanak.

The affair was, in the end, settled peacefully, with the Turks agreeing to respect the
neutrality of Chanak and the surrounding
district. But the old question was again
asked — was Churchill too ready to risk war?

Lost election

The Conservatives left the Coalition in October
1922 and Lloyd George had to resign as
Prime Minister. Churchill, recovering from an
operation, could visit his own constituency,
Dundee, only late in the campaign. He stood
as a Liberal and lost his seat, finding himself,
as he later recorded:

> without an office, without a seat, without
> a party and without an appendix.

Chapter Five 1924-1929

The Conservative Chancellor

Churchill lost two more elections in 1923 and in March 1924 before he regained a place in Parliament. His Labour opponent in March 1924 described how, when the votes were being counted and Churchill knew he was defeated,

> he began to tramp the length of the hall, head down, body lurching, like a despairing animal.

Churchill's dislike of the first Labour government which came into office in January 1924 with Liberal support, brought him nearer to the Conservatives. In October 1924 he stood, with Conservative support, as a "Constitutionalist" at Epping, and won the seat. The Conservatives won the election and the new Prime Minister, Baldwin, had to decide whether to include this brilliant but still unpopular new supporter, Churchill, in the Cabinet. Tom Jones gave advice:

> I would certainly have him inside, not out. He is incapable of being permanently loyal to anybody but Winston, and you must count on your loyal men to withstand him.

On 5 November Baldwin discussed with Neville Chamberlain the question of who

19 Churchill follows the Prime Minister, Stanley Baldwin (bottom right) out of 10, Downing Street during the 1926 Imperial Conference.

should be Chancellor of the Exchequer — a very important post. Chamberlain recorded

> He mentioned Winston but said he supposed there would be a howl from the party. I said I thought there would, but that would be so if he came in [to the government] at all, and I did not know if it would be much louder if he went to the Treasury [i.e. became Chancellor] . . .

Baldwin took the risk. He told Tom Jones:

> The Treasury officials in the old days used to tell me that they believed Winston would make a good Chancellor. Then it would be a good thing to keep him fully occupied with finance . . . . Lastly, having decided to bring him into the Cabinet, to give him the Chancellorship would be bound to remove every possible personal grievance. It would be up to him to be loyal, if he is capable of loyalty.

Baldwin saw Churchill and asked him if he would take office "as Chancellor". "Of the Duchy?" asked Churchill, thinking of the minor post of Chancellor of the Duchy of Lancaster. "No, of the Exchequer", said Baldwin. Churchill had always wanted this office, which his father had held. He told Baldwin "You have done more for me than Lloyd George ever did."

Soon Churchill formally rejoined the Conservative party. The Liberal newspaper, the *Manchester Guardian,* commented:

> Mr Churchill for the second time has — shall we say — quitted the sinking ship, and for the second time the reward of this fine instinct has been not safety only but high promotion.

Economic policies

Churchill wanted to make Britain prosperous and reduce unemployment. A cut in income tax would, he thought, leave people with more money to invest in industry — and to spend on British goods. Tax cuts meant cuts in government spending, and Churchill now opposed defence spending. J.C.C. Davidson, Parliamentary Secretary to the Admiralty, later wrote:

> It was characteristic of Winston Churchill that he put the whole of his energy into what he believed to be the right policy of the Department over which he presided. When he was at the Exchequer he believed that he was the keeper of the public purse and must keep a most severe control over all spending departments. And, although an old First Lord of the Admiralty, he felt compelled to oppose the expenditure regarded as the minimum required by the Navy . . . . This led to a first-class row . . .

Beatty, the First Sea Lord, nearly exploded:

> That extraordinary fellow Winston has gone mad. Economically mad, and no sacrifice is too great to achieve . . . 1/- [5p] off the Income Tax. Nobody outside a lunatic asylum expects a shilling off the Income Tax this Budget. But he has made up his mind that it is the only thing he can do to justify his appointment as Chancellor of the Exchequer . . .

Churchill over-rode all arguments, including references to possible danger in the Far East from Japan:

> A war with Japan! But why should there be a war with Japan? I do not believe there is the slightest chance of it in our lifetime.

Baldwin in the end worked out a compromise. Still, in his April 1925 budget the Chancellor reduced income tax by 6d [2½p], to 4/- [20p] in the pound. He also announced a scheme for widows' pensions, and for old-age pensions to be paid at age 65 (instead of 70).

Back to the Gold Standard

Many Treasury experts thought it would add to Britain's reputation if British currency

had a fixed value in gold, as it had done before 1914. They convinced Churchill of this and in May 1925 Britain went "back on the Gold Standard", with the value of the pound fixed at 4.86 dollars. This turned out to be a mistake, as it sent up the price of British exports and helped to cause even more unemployment. One economic expert, Maynard Keynes, disagreed with the policy. He wrote a pamphlet called *The Economic Consequences of Mr. Churchill*. Although Churchill was later much blamed for taking Britain back onto the Gold Standard, he had been, as Keynes said, "gravely misled by his experts".

The General Strike, 1926

A miners' strike against a reduction of their wages led other unions to promise support. On the night of 2 May 1926 discussions between the government and the Trades Union Congress broke down, and a General Strike began. Churchill was sympathetic to the miners, but not to the unions' attempt to

put pressure on the government. He told Tom Jones on 4 May:

> There are two disputes on: there is the General Strike which is a challenge to the Government and with which we cannot compromise . . . . There is also a trade dispute in the coal industry: on that we are prepared to take the utmost pains to reach a settlement . . .

Once the contest between government and unions began, Churchill was determined to win. Baldwin, who was very anxious for the dispute to end peacefully, was glad to accept a suggestion that Churchill should edit a government newspaper, *The British Gazette*:

> Yes. It will keep him busy and stop him doing worse things.

The British Gazette

Published by His Majesty's Stationery Office.

No. 5.   LONDON, MONDAY, MAY 10, 1926.   ONE PENNY.

VITAL SERVICES BETTER EACH DAY.

Obstruction By Pickets More Effectually Overcome.

FREE MOVEMENT OF CONVOYS IN THE LONDON DOCK AREA.

Civil Authorities Suppress Disorder Without Aid Of Troops.

OFFICIAL COMMUNIQUE.

May 9.

The general situation is unchanged. On the whole, throughout England, the attempted obstruction by pickets to the movement of necessary supplies has weakened and is being more effectually overcome.

There has been a recrudescence of rioting at Hull, and a somewhat considerable riot occurred last night at Middlesbrough. In both cases the disorder was suppressed and numerous arrests were made.

Attempts to interrupt the convoys on the London-Thames Haven-road were marked by stone throwing and bottle throwing. Strong reinforcements were available, and this route will be brought under strict control.

Complete confidence and order are maintained throughout the London dock area. Convoys are moving freely in and out of the docks. The work of loading and unloading vessels by volunteer labour is proceeding and increasing continually.

No difficulty is experienced in the re-victualling of London, and it is intended to keep the Port of London regularly opened. In general the situation at all the ports is distinctly better than last week.

MR. BALDWIN AND THE NATION.

A Confident Appeal.

NO SURRENDER ON VITAL ISSUE.

Mr. Baldwin, the Prime Minister, on Saturday evening broadcast the following message to the nation :—

The General Strike has now been in progress for nearly a week, and I think it is right that as Prime Minister I should tell the nation once more what is at stake in the lamentable struggle that is going on.

There are two distinct issues—the stoppage in the coal industry and the General Strike. The stoppage in the coal industry has followed nine months' inquiry and negotiations. I did my utmost to secure agreement upon the basis of the Commission's report, and when the time comes, as I hope it soon may, to discuss the terms upon which the coal industry is to be carried on, I shall continue my efforts to see that in any settlement justice is done both to the miners and the owners.

What, then, is the issue for which the Government is fighting ? It is fighting because, while negotiations were still in progress, the Trade Union Council ordered a General Strike, presumably to try to force Parliament and the community to bend to its will.

With that object, the Trade Union Council has decreed that the railways shall not run, that transport shall not move, that the unloading of ships shall stop, and that no news shall reach the public. The supply of electricity and the transportation of food supplies to the people have been interrupted. The Trade Union Council declares that this is merely an industrial dispute, but their method of helping the miners is to attack the community. Can there be a more direct attack upon the community than a body, not elected by the voters of the country, without consulting the people, without consulting even the Trade Unionists, and in order to impose conditions never yet defined, should dislocate the life of the nation and try to starve us into submission.

THE MINING DISPUTE.

TO ALL WORKERS IN ALL TRADES.

Additional Guarantees.

Official.

Every man who does his duty by the country and remains at work or returns to work during the present crisis will be protected by the State from loss of trade union benefits, superannuation allowances, or pension. His Majesty's Government will take whatever steps are necessary in Parliament or otherwise for this purpose.

STANLEY BALDWIN.

POSTAL SERVICES.

Very Little Delay in Letter Deliveries.

The mail services as a whole are working satisfactorily. There is no actual stoppage on main routes, and when necessary mails are forwarded by road and the proportion sent by rail continues to increase.

Letters from London are being delivered in nearly all the towns in the midlands and the south of England on the day following postage, while letters from London to Edinburgh and Glasgow are reaching their destinations on the second day.

From to-day the services will be further expedited.

NEWS FROM THE DISTRICTS

Chief Trades Almost Normal.

INDUSTRY IN MIDLANDS.

Engineering Works Busy.

Encouraging week-end reports come from some of the chief industrial towns in the Midlands. Brief surveys of the position are given below :

LEICESTER.—The situation is almost normal. Production has been very little interfered with, and there has been no friction between the various unions and the employers. Full production is being maintained in the engineering trades, and no engineers have been called out, with the exception of those on of one firm whose men came out on Tuesday but returned to work almost immediately. The boot and hosiery trades are working half-time by mutual arrangement. This restriction has been necessary owing to the anticipated difficulty of clearing stocks, and not to shortage of fuel or power. The hosiery trades at Loughborough are on full time with the exception of one firm, but the industries in and around Hinckley are on half time for the same reasons as those which apply at Leicester. Transport difficulties are being overcome and efficient volunteer services are running. The local paper is being printed, and *The British Gazette* is on sale at 9 a.m.

NOTTINGHAM.—A section of the engineers are on strike. Attempts were made to bring out the hosiery workers and the employees of the Raleigh Cycle Company. They were unsuccessful. Hose pipes were brought into play when attempts were made to bring out the workers at Players' tobacco factory. Lace firms are mainly closed, but this has been the case for some time owing to bad trade. Transport is at a standstill and the strikers are trying to prevent the working of the volunteer services. There has been a good deal of hooligan-

LORD BALFOUR DEFINES THE ISSUE.

Attempted Revolution—Its Purpose And Results.

"The Civilisation Of Which We Are Trustees"

Two hundred and thirty-eight years have passed since a revolution occurred in this country, whose object was to secure the supremacy of Parliamentary Government, and the traditional liberties of our people.

Through eight generations it has proved successful. But we are now threatened, it seems, with a revolution of a very dierent kind ; and it behoves us seriously to consider what are its practical methods, what are its avowed objects, what would be its actual results were it unhappily to succeed.

Its methods are being practised before our eyes. They are to deprive the people of food, transport, employment, and a free Press.

The conveniences of civilised life, which have long been counted among its necessities, are in some cases to be immensely diminished, in others to be brought to an end. Personal security is to be threatened. Industry is to be seriously hampered, even when it is not wholly stopped. Willing workers are to be kept in idleness ; anxious purchasers are to be kept in want ; perishable food is to rot in part ; all the wheels of social life are to be clogged.

Such are the methods of the revolutionary movement ; what, then, are its objects ?

The British Gazette

Churchill wrote for the paper, using very extreme language (he even talked about the strikers as "the enemy"). J.C.C. Davidson, who supervised the scheme, objected to some of his articles:

> After a great fight, Winston agreed to be blue-pencilled, and from that moment my blue pencil was seldom idle.

Others who worked on the paper found Churchill a great trial. Tom Jones reported from Downing Street:

> Gwynne of the 'Morning Post' has sent several messages begging that Winston should be kept away from that office where the 'British Gazette' is being printed. He butts in at the busiest hours and insists on changing commas and full stops until the staff is furious.

Davidson wrote crossly:

> He thinks he is Napoleon, but curiously enough the men who have been printing all their life in the various processes happen to know more about their job than he does.

Beaverbrook, who had a fierce quarrel with Churchill at this time, commented:

> Churchill on top of the wave has in him the stuff of which tyrants are made.

The Trade Unionists, who abandoned the strike after ten days, felt that *The British Gazette* had been very unfair to them. They did not forgive or forget Churchill's attitude. As Lord Shinwell later wrote:

> The mention of his name at Labour gatherings was the signal for derisive cheers; when a Labour speaker found himself short of arguments, he only had to say 'Down with Winston Churchill'. This never failed to draw thunderous applause.

Attitude to the miners

When the miners stayed out on strike, Churchill showed his best side by working harder than anyone to get a good settlement for the men from the coal-owners. Jones noted in September 1926 that he

> was quite prepared to go to great lengths in the way of legislation on hours, wages, and conditions — which terrified his colleagues.

He was always ready to be generous once his side had won. Unfortunately, he was not successful in negotiating good terms in this case — though as late as 1929 miners' leaders were still talking about "how Winston had nearly pulled off a settlement" in the dispute.

Reputation as Chancellor

Baldwin and the Conservatives lost the election in 1929, and Churchill became the ex-Chancellor of the Exchequer. A fair comment on his success in the job was made later by Robert Boothby:

> His output was colossal. He was basically uninterested in the problems of high finance. But his Budgets were skilfully contrived and superbly presented. And given the conditions under which he was obliged to work . . . he could hardly have done better, or other than he did.

Churchill impressed Baldwin too. In 1936 Baldwin told some friends:

> You can say what you like about Winston, but I tell you that man can work — and how he can work.

◁ 22   Churchill and his wife campaigning in relaxed fashion during the 1929 election.

Chapter Six   1929-1939

In the Wilderness

In spite of his solid work as Chancellor of the Exchequer, Churchill was still unpopular. The *Times* in March 1931 remarked:

> . . . it is difficult to imagine MR CHURCHILL in the role of a leader acceptable to the mass of the Conservative party.

India

In 1930 Churchill quarrelled with Baldwin over India. Baldwin wanted British-ruled India to be given a definite promise of dominion status, with self-government, one day, and he supported the new Labour government over this. Churchill did not think Indians were ready for independence. He had written to a friend in 1922:

> Our true duty in India lies to those 300 millions whose lives and means of existence would be squandered if entrusted to the chatterboxes who are supposed to speak for India today.

Churchill's attitude to India was protective and kindly. Baldwin scored a good point against him in a debate in the Commons, by quoting an earlier speech of Churchill's own, in which he had said:

> Our reign in India or anywhere else has never stood on the basis of physical force alone, and it would be fatal to the British Empire if we were to try to base ourselves

only upon it [i.e. on force]. The British way of doing things . . . has always meant and implied close and effectual cooperation with the people of the country . . .

However, Churchill did not realize that Indians now wanted more control over their own lives. He campaigned furiously and warned the British that any weakening of their power in India might lead to bloodshed. He spoke in Manchester in January 1931:

> If, guided by counsels of madness and cowardice disguised as false benevolence, you troop home from India, you will leave behind you what John Morley called 'a bloody chaos' . . .

When negotiations with the Indian leader Gandhi took place in 1931, Churchill horrified progressive Conservatives by saying that it was

> alarming and also nauseating to see Mr. Gandhi, a seditious Middle Temple lawyer, now posing as a fakir of a type well known in the East, striding half-naked up the steps of the Viceregal Palace, while he is still organising and conducting a defiant campaign of civil disobedience . . .

Hostility to Churchill

From January 1931 Churchill was a back-

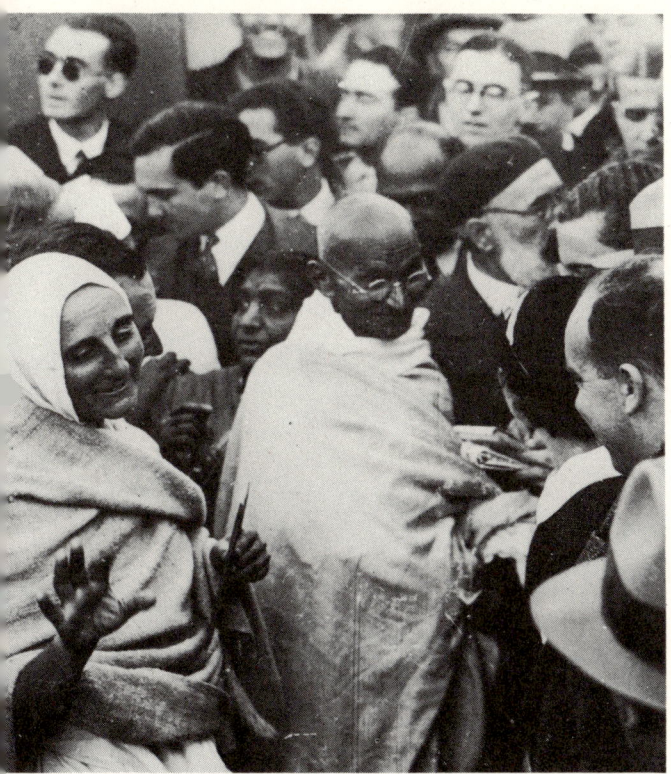

23 The Indian leader Gandhi on a visit to England in 1931.

bench MP, having resigned from the "Shadow Cabinet" of the day when Baldwin agreed to work out a constitution for India together with the Labour government. Other MPs complained that Churchill was completely wrapped up in his own enthusiasms, especially in his ideas about India. The Labour leader George Lansbury protested in May 1932:

He never listens to any other man's speech but his own.

There was no attempt to find a place for Churchill in any government, not even when Baldwin became Prime Minister again in 1935. Churchill's friend Brendan Bracken later remembered how

. . . in his years in the wilderness . . . he kept saying: 'I'm finished'. He said that about twice a day. He was quite certain that he would never get back to office, for everyone seemed to regard him as a wild man.

Other people thought he was finished too. Beaverbrook, part friend and part rival, wrote to the editor of the *Observer* in January 1932 that Churchill

has held every view on every question. He has been apparently quite sincere in all his views. Perhaps he has convinced himself. But he is utterly unreliable in his mental attitude.

In January 1934 Beaverbrook's comment was:

I think Winston Churchill will retire from Parliament. It is really the best thing for him to do.

The Abdication

What Beaverbrook described as "perhaps the blackest day in Churchill's personal career in politics, along with the day he was dismissed from the Admiralty", came when Churchill tried to defend Edward VIII at the time of the crisis over the King's wish to marry a divorced woman, Mrs Simpson. The Prime Minister, Baldwin, and many ordinary British people disapproved of such a marriage for the King, and Edward VIII decided to abdicate (give up his throne). Churchill felt Baldwin had forced the King to make this decision. Harold Nicolson, a fellow MP, described in a letter Churchill's attempt to speak in the House of Commons in favour of giving the King more time to consider:

7 December 1936
House of Commons

. . . Winston (whose line is, 'let the King choose his girl') suffered an utter defeat. He almost lost his head, and he certainly lost his command of the House. It was terribly dramatic.

First we had Baldwin — slow and measured. Then Winston rose to ask a supplementary question. He failed to do it in the right form and was twice called to order by the Speaker. He hesitated and waved

24 Like Churchill, this man is on his own in his demonstration in favour of Edward VIII. Public opinion generally was against any marriage between the King and Mrs Simpson.

his spectacles vaguely in the air. 'Sit down' they shouted. He waved his spectacles again and then collapsed. It was almost painful.

Germany

Because Churchill was known for his extreme and eccentric views, no one would listen when he had something really valuable to say. Since 1933 he had warned the House of Commons that Hitler's Germany was dangerous to Britain. He reminded them in a speech on 22 February 1938:

In those days I ventured repeatedly to submit to the House the maxim that the grievances of the vanquished [Germany] should be redressed before the disarmament of the victors was begun. But the reverse was done . . .

After Germany re-occupied the Rhineland in 1936, the British government did decide to spend more on defence (£158 million was allocated for 1936-37). Churchill welcomed this. However, early in 1938 Hitler annexed Austria. Churchill redoubled his warnings:

Austria has been laid in thrall, and we do not know whether Czechoslovakia will not suffer a similar attack . . . . I predict that the day will come when at some point or other on some issue or other you will have to make a stand . . .

He was still looked on with suspicion. After all, said some MPs, Churchill had *cut* defence spending in the 1920s (though under very different circumstances). One young friend, a Conservative MP, Anthony Crossley, wrote sympathetic verses in Churchill's defence. For example,

. . . *You're polite to the small and you're rude to the great:*
Your opinions are bolder and surer
Than is seemly today in an office of state —
You've even insulted the Führer

Baldwin had retired as Prime Minister in May 1937 and was succeeded by Neville Chamberlain. In 1938 Baldwin warned Anthony Eden, who had resigned as Foreign Secretary after disagreements with Chamberlain, not to work too closely with Churchill. Baldwin wrote to a friend of Eden:

Tell A [Anthony] . . . not to be dominated by W [Winston] and play second fiddle to him.

Yet Baldwin still recognized Churchill's abilities. In the same letter, he commented:

W is a very forceful character and if war should come, the country will want him to lead them.

The Munich Crisis

War nearly came in the autumn of 1938, when Hitler demanded the Sudetenland from Czechoslovakia. France was bound by treaty to help Czechoslovakia if she were attacked, and if France went to war with Germany, it would be difficult for Britain to stand aside. Chamberlain visited Germany and avoided war by a compromise — the Munich Agreement, which allowed Hitler to occupy the Sudetenland. Churchill was one of the small number of MPs who refused to welcome the settlement reached at Munich. He explained why in the House of Commons on 5 October 1938:

Mr Churchill: If I do not begin this afternoon by paying the usual, and indeed almost invariable tributes to the Prime Minister for his handling of this crisis, it is certainly not from any lack of personal regard. We have always, over a great many years, had very pleasant relations, and I have deeply understood from personal experience of my own in a similar crisis the stress and strain he has had to bear; but I am sure it is much better to say

25 Churchill strongly opposed the agreement made by Neville Chamberlain (walking second-right in this picture) with Adolf Hitler (second left) at Munich in September 1938.

exactly what we think about public affairs, and this is certainly not the time when it is worth anyone's while to court political popularity . . . . I will, therefore, begin by saying the most unpopular and unwelcome thing. I will begin by saying what everybody would like to ignore or forget but which must nevertheless be stated, namely, that we have sustained a total and unmitigated defeat, and that France has suffered even more than we have.

Viscountess Astor: Nonsense.

Mr Churchill: When the Noble Lady cries 'Nonsense', she could not have heard . . . just now that Herr Hitler had gained in this particular leap forward in substance all he set out to gain. The utmost my right hon. Friend the Prime Minister has been able to secure by all his immense exertions . . . has been that the German dictator, instead of snatching his victuals from the table, has been content to have them served to him course by course.

Lady Astor was not the only one to interrupt. Churchill later wrote:

> I well remember that when I said "We have sustained a total and unmitigated defeat" the storm which met me made it necessary to pause for a while before resuming . . . . The House [of Commons] approved the policy of His Majesty's Government "by which war was averted in the recent crisis" by 366 to 144. The thirty or forty dissentient Conservatives could do no more than register their disapproval by abstention. This we did as a formal and united act.

The dissenters remained in their seats when everyone else went out to vote.

On 9 October 1938 Hitler said in a public speech:

> It only needs that in England instead of Chamberlain, Mr. Duff Cooper [who had resigned over Munich] or Mr. Eden or Mr. Churchill should come to power, and then we know quite well that it would be the aim of these men immediately to begin a new World War. They make no secret of the fact: they admit it openly . . .

The "old lion"

Churchill continued to speak out, although he was accused of being a "war-monger" in England too. He had to defend himself in his own constituency of Epping — and told his constituents in 1939:

> People talk about our parliamentary institutions and parliamentary democracy; but if these are to survive, it will not be because the constituencies return tame, docile, subservient members, and try to keep out every form of independent judgment.

However, by the spring of 1939, public opinion was swinging towards the view that Churchill was right after all. In March Hitler took the rest of his "victuals", just as Churchill had said he would — he occupied what was left of Czechoslovakia. Britain joined France in promising to protect Poland and Roumania, two other countries threatened by Hitler's ambitions. On 19 May Churchill stressed the need for Britain and France to make an alliance with Russia if effective help were to be given to Poland (the Bolsheviks, he had decided, were not as bad as Hitler — or rather, they were less dangerous to Britain):

> I beg His Majesty's Government to get some of these brutal truths into their heads. Without any effective Eastern front, there can be no satisfactory defence of our interests in the West, and without Russia there can be no effective Eastern front . . .

He was now listened to with more respect in the House of Commons as well as in the country as a whole. Harold Nicolson's diary records this change in attitude:

> 19 April 1939
> The feeling that Winston is essential is gaining strength, and we shall probably see him in the cabinet within a short time.

In August 1939 Churchill, still not included in the government, opposed the adjournment of Parliament for the summer break, in view of the situation in Europe. Harold Nicolson wrote to his wife on 2 August:

> We have a debate today about whether we should adjourn or not. I had hoped that Anthony Eden was going to take a strong line, but he is now suggesting that we should all toe the line [and agree to adjournment]. I would do so were it not that Winston refuses, and I cannot let the old lion enter the lobby [to vote against the government] alone.

Before the end of August Parliament was hastily recalled.

Chapter Seven 1939-1940

The War Leader
— Saving Britain

War was declared on 3 September 1939. The Prime Minister, Chamberlain, had already decided that Churchill was needed in a wartime government. He now offered him the Admiralty and a place in the War Cabinet. Churchill lost no time. He later wrote:

> . . . the opening hours of war may be vital with navies. I therefore sent word to the Admiralty that I would take charge forthwith and arrive at 6 o'clock. On this the Board were kind enough to signal to the Fleet, 'Winston is back'. So it was that I came again to the room I had quitted in pain and sorrow almost exactly a quarter of a century before . . .

The fall of Chamberlain

In May 1940 the failure of a British expedition to Norway, with which Churchill had been much involved, led to a demand for changes in the government. This time, however, it was the Prime Minister, not the First Lord of the Admiralty, who was attacked. The war was going badly and Chamberlain seemed too weak for a war-leader. A national government, including all parties, was needed, and Labour MPs would not join one which was headed by Chamberlain. Robert Boothby later wrote:

> . . . in May 1940, the House of Commons at last faced up to its responsibilities, and dismissed the Chamberlain government, after a tense and dramatic debate.
> This was the single decisive vote I cast during my thirty-four years as a Member of Parliament. I was one of thirty-three Conservatives who voted against the Government we had been elected to support. Others abstained. And the result was that, although the Government obtained a majority, it was not of sufficient size to command public confidence in the greatest crisis of our history.
> Mr. Chamberlain resigned . . .

Churchill becomes Prime Minister

Lord Halifax, not Churchill, was the favourite to succeed Chamberlain. But Halifax decided that it would be difficult for him, as a member of the House of Lords, to be Prime Minister. On 10 May the King sent for Churchill. When the new Prime Minister returned from Buckingham Palace he told his bodyguard, W.H. Thompson, of his appointment. Thompson replied:

> I am very pleased that at last you have become Prime Minister sir, but I only wish that the position had come your way in better times, for you have taken on an enormous task.

Not everyone was pleased. One civil servant, Colville, later recorded:

◁ 26 The *Daily Mail* cartoon for 13 May 1940 — Churchill was now Minister of Defence as well as Prime Minister.

policy? I will say: It is to wage war, by sea, land and air, with all our might and with all the strength that God can give us: to wage war against a monstrous tyranny, never surpassed in the dark, lamentable catalogue of human crime. That is our policy. You ask, what is our aim? I can answer in one word: Victory — victory at all costs, victory in spite of all terror, victory, however long and hard the road may be . . .

Churchill formed his new government from members of all parties. He included many of the old Conservative ministers, including Chamberlain. Past mistakes, he told the House of Commons on 18 June, must be forgotten:

There are many who would hold an inquest in the House of Commons on the conduct of the Governments — and of Parliaments, for they are in it too — during the years which led up to this catastrophe . . . . This . . . would be a foolish and pernicious process. There are too many in it . . .

Later, Churchill spoke in praise of Chamberlain's unselfish attitude during the changeover of power. He remembered on 12 November 1940:

I had the singular experience of passing in a day from being one of his most prominent opponents and critics to being one of his principal lieutenants, and on another day of passing from serving under him to become the head of a Government of which, with perfect loyalty, he was content to be a member. Such relationships are unusual in our public life.

Dunkirk

In June 1940 the German advance threatened to cut off all the British forces in Europe.

In May 1940 the mere thought of Churchill as Prime Minister sent a cold chill down the spines of the staff of 10 Downing Street . . . . Our feelings . . . were widely shared in the Cabinet offices, the Treasury and Whitehall.

The "darkest hours"

The Germans had invaded Belgium and Holland on the day of Chamberlain's resignation, and soon they had advanced far into France. On 13 May 1940, in his first speech in the House of Commons as Prime Minister, Churchill made clear both the dangers Britain faced and his government's determination to overcome them:

I would say to the House, as I said to those who have joined this Government: 'I have nothing to offer but blood, toil, tears and sweat' . . . . You ask what is our

Churchill, in between trips to France to encourage his allies, had to make painful decisions. Robert Boothby related a conversation with Churchill, who remembered one such decision:

"I did Calais myself. I personally gave the order to stand and fight it out to the end. I agreed to the evacuation of Boulogne with reluctance; and I think now that I ought to have ordered them to fight it out there too. But the order to Calais meant certain death for almost the entire garrison.

It was the only time during the war that I couldn't eat. I was very nearly sick at dinner". Tears came into his eyes. "But . . . it gave us two vital days."

At the time Churchill explained to the House of Commons about the soldiers who had died defending Calais:

Their sacrifice . . . was not in vain. At least two [German] armoured divisions, which otherwise would have been turned against the British Expeditionary Force [the main body of British troops], had to be sent to overcome them . . . and the time gained enabled the Gravelines waterlines to be flooded and to be held by the French troops. Thus it was that the port of Dunkirk was kept open . . .

Through Dunkirk many British soldiers were evacuated. Earlier there had been fears that they might all be lost. Churchill told the House of Commons the story on 4 June:

A miracle of deliverance . . . is manifest to us all. The enemy was hurled back by the retreating British and French troops . . . . The Royal Air Force engaged the main strength of the German Air Force, and inflicted upon them losses of at least four to one; and the Navy, using nearly 1,000 ships of all kinds, carried over 335,000 men, French and British, out of the jaws of death and shame . . .

27 A German photograph of allied soldiers who failed to escape from Dunkirk. Its title was "Victorious Retreat". Churchill himself warned 'Wars are not won by evacuations".

He went on to speak plainly about the real meaning of the Dunkirk rescue:

We must be very careful not to assign to this deliverance the attributes of a victory. Wars are not won by evacuations . . . our thankfulness at the escape of our Army . . . must not blind us to the fact that what has happened in France and Belgium is a colossal military disaster . . .

Finally, it was vital to make clear that whatever happened in Europe, Britain would not surrender:

I have, myself, full confidence that if all do their duty . . . we shall prove ourselves once again able to defend our island home, to ride out the storm of war, and to outlive the menace of tyranny, if necessary for years, if necessary alone. At any rate, that is what we are going to try to do . . . . We shall go on to the end, we shall fight in France, we shall fight on the seas and oceans, we shall fight with growing confidence and growing strength in the air, we shall defend our island, whatever the cost may be, we shall fight in the fields, and in the streets, we shall fight in the hills; we shall never surrender . . .

The fall of France

On 17 June 1940 Churchill in a short broadcast gave the worst news of the war — that France was likely to make a separate peace with Germany:

The news from France is very bad and I grieve for the gallant French people who have fallen into this terrible misfortune. Nothing will alter our feelings towards them or our faith that the genius of France will rise again. What has happened in France makes no difference to our actions and purpose.

These two points — no attempt to pile blame on the French for surrendering to the Germans, but a clear statement that Britain would fight on — were made again in speeches throughout June and July. On 18 June to the House of Commons (and later in a broadcast) Churchill said:

What General Weygand called the Battle of France is over. I expect that the Battle of Britain is about to begin . . . . The whole fury and might of the enemy must very soon be turned on us. Hitler knows that he will have to break us in this island or lose the war. If we can stand up to him, all Europe may be free . . . . But if we fail, then the whole world, including the United States, including all that we have known and cared for, will sink into the abyss of a new dark age . . . . Let us therefore brace ourselves to our duties, and so bear ourselves that, if the British Empire and its

Commonwealth last for a thousand years, men will still say "This was their finest hour".

In notes made for a speech in a secret session of the House of Commons on 20 June 1940 Churchill made his points again:

Melancholy position of the French Government.
We have to make the best of them.
No criticisms, no recriminations.
    We cannot afford it, in public.

and also:

If Hitler fails to invade
    or destroy Britain
        he has lost the war . . .
If get through next 3 months
    get through next 3 years.

France surrendered to Germany on 22 June 1940. Preparations for defence against an invasion of Britain went ahead. In a world broadcast on 14 July 1940 Churchill spoke of the country's determination to resist:

Should the invader come to Britain, there will be no placid lying down of the people in submission before him as we have seen, alas, in other countries. We shall defend every village, every town, and every city. The vast mass of London itself, fought street by street, could easily devour an entire hostile army; and we would rather see London laid in ruins and ashes than that it should be tamely and abjectly enslaved . . .

Hitler commented on 19 July 1940:

. . . Churchill has said that he will fight on . . . now I realize the continuation of this war means the destruction of one or the other of the adversaries. Churchill thinks it is going to be Germany. But I think it is going to be Britain.

The French fleet

Churchill had another painful decision to

make after the collapse of France. There was uncertainty as to what would happen to the French Navy: would the Germans take over the French ships? In fact, French commanders had been told to sink their ships rather than hand them over to the Germans, but the British did not know this. Churchill ordered the British Navy to take control of all French fighting-ships on 3 July. The French fleet at Oran resisted and so the British destroyed it. On 4 July Churchill told the House of Commons:

> It is with sincere sorrow that I must now announce to the House the measures which we have felt bound to take in order to prevent the French Fleet from falling into German hands . . . . I fear the loss of life among the French and in the harbour [of Oran] must have been very heavy . . .

MPs of all parties applauded this speech and the decision to take over the French ships, not because they were not sorry for the French but because they felt Churchill had been right not to risk a German take-over of the French Navy. Churchill felt the matter deeply, however. His friend Lord Beaverbrook saw him just after he had given the order to fire if necessary on the French at Oran. They walked together in the early hours of the morning in the garden of 10 Downing Street. Beaverbrook wrote:

> There was a high wind blowing. He raced along, I had trouble keeping up with him . . . . Churchill declared that there was no other decision possible. Then he wept.

Reinforcements for Egypt

A less painful but very important decision had to be made in August 1940. At a time when German invasion of Britain was still feared Churchill and his War Cabinet decided to take the risk of sending 154 precious tanks to Egypt to reinforce British troops there. Of this, Churchill himself later wrote:

> It is odd that while at the time everyone

28   One of "the few": a Hurricane fighter takes off in 1940.

concerned was quite calm and cheerful, writing about it afterwards makes one shudder.

The Battle of Britain

The Battle of Britain turned out to be an air battle. British 'planes prevented the Germans from gaining control of the air which they needed in order to launch an invasion. On 20 August 1940 Churchill reported to the House of Commons:

> The great air battle which has been in progress over this island for the last few weeks has recently attained a high intensity . . . . The gratitude of every home in our island, in our Empire, and indeed throughout the world, except in the abodes of the guilty, goes out to the British airmen who, undaunted by odds, unwearied in their constant challenge and mortal danger, are turning the tide of the world war by their powers and by their devotion. Never in the field of human conflict was so much owed by so many to so few.

On 17 September Hitler postponed any invasion "until further notice" and on 12 October he cancelled any attempt in 1940.

29   In September 1940 Churchill strides through the bombed City of London.

The "Blitz"

Heavy bombing of London began on 7 September 1940. Churchill often visited bombed areas. Lord Ismay later described a visit to the London docks:

> 'Good old Winnie', they cried. 'We thought you'd come and see us. We can take it. Give it 'em back'. Churchill broke down, and as I was struggling to get him through the crowd, I heard an old woman say 'You see, he really cares. He's crying.' Having pulled himself together he proceeded to march through dockland at break neck speed.

Churchill told the House of Commons in October:

> in all my life, I have never been treated with so much kindness as by the people who have suffered most. One would think one had brought some great benefit to them, instead of the blood and tears, the toil and sweat which is all I have ever promised.

He saw to it that more generous compensation was paid to the people who lost houses or shops through air-raids.

The USA

Churchill built up a close relationship with President Roosevelt of the USA. He knew that American help was vital to Britain. On 20 August 1940 he announced in Parliament an arrangement to lease bases in British colonies to the United States:

> Undoubtedly this process means that these two great organizations . . . the British Empire and the United States, will have to be somewhat mixed up together in some of their affairs . . . . I do not view the process with any misgivings. I could not stop it if I wished, no one can stop it. Like the Mississippi, it just keeps rolling along.

Soon, Roosevelt persuaded the Americans to let Britain buy vital materials like steel, and pay the bills later.

Chapter Eight 1941-1944

The War Leader
—Fighting a World War

Churchill had to work hard during the war to keep up British morale. John G. Winant, the American Ambassador, wrote to Roosevelt in April 1941:

> The Prime Minister's method of conducting a campaign on what one might call a morale front is unique. He arrives at a town unannounced, is taken to the most seriously bombed area, leaves his automobile and starts walking through the streets without guards. The news of his presence spreads rapidly by word of mouth and before he has gone far crowds flock about him and people call out to him, 'Hello, Winnie', 'Good old Winnie', 'You will never let us down', 'That's a man'.

Hitler complained of Churchill's obstinate determination to fight on:

> It was not possible to come to an understanding with this enemy. The English are lunatics, blindfolded people . . . . He [Churchill] wanted the war and now he has got it. All offers [of peace, on Hitler's terms] were repelled by the war-monger Churchill. He took all my offers as weakness . . .

Broadcasts

Churchill continued to broadcast stirring speeches. Robert Wood, the BBC engineer in charge of outside broadcasts, has described their effect:

30 Churchill, in his comfortable one-piece "siren-suit", makes a wartime broadcast from 10 Downing Street.

> . . . I would listen to him speak and, when he'd finished, I would find that we hadn't had it after all, we still had a fighting chance, and come what may we were going to win. It was an extraordinary achievement.

45

31 Although he looks suitably angry here at the news of the Japanese attack on the USA in December 1941, Churchill was glad to have the Americans in the war.

[the Greeks] all the aid in our power.

Then an attempt to defend the island of Crete failed, and there was another evacuation on 27 May. On 10 June 1941 Churchill defended himself against criticism in the House of Commons:

> Defeat is bitter. There is no use in trying to explain defeat. People do not like defeat, and they do not like the explanations . . . . For defeat there is only one answer. The only answer to defeat is victory. If a Government in time of war gives the impression that it cannot in the long run procure victory, who cares for its explanations? It ought to go — that is to say, if you are quite sure you can find another which can do better.

Practically no one thought Churchill's government should go — as Churchill well knew. After the Greek defeat, the Commons had voted by 447 to 3 to continue to support him.

The German attack on Russia

On 22 June 1941 Churchill heard that Germany had invaded Russia. Britain was no longer alone. Churchill accepted Russia as an ally — even Bolsheviks were better than no ally at all. Just before the invasion, Churchill had told his secretary Colville:

> If Hitler invaded Hell, I would at least make a favourable reference to the Devil in the House of Commons.

Now he made a world broadcast:

> The Russian danger is . . . our danger and the danger of the United States, just as the cause of any Russian fighting for his hearth and home is the cause of free men and free peoples in every quarter of the globe.

Wood did not find Churchill easy to handle:

> I used to have to listen to his speeches very carefully, for he was a great one for adding a bit on at the end. He would say in rehearsal, 'This is how I'll end'. But when he was wound up he often found more to say, and heaven help me if I'd cut him off before he'd finished . . . . He was a devil to work for, but a treat to work with, because he made you feel Britain was getting somewhere at last.

Failure in Greece

Churchill had to tell the British people about many defeats before any successes came. In Greece, British troops sent to help against an expected German invasion had to be rapidly evacuated in April 1941. Twelve thousand men and much equipment were lost. Some people thought that the men should never have been sent, especially since they were needed in North Africa. Churchill told the House of Commons:

> We were bound in honour to give them

In practice, Churchill realized that little could be done to help Russia except by sending her supplies. He had learnt caution. In July 1941 he told guests of Anthony Eden:

Remember that on my breast are the medals of the Dardanelles, Antwerp . . . and Greece, and I cannot support any more adventures or expeditions like that . . .

The Far East

Even a Prime Minister as alert and hard-working as Churchill could not give equal attention to all areas. The Far East, where Japan was building up her military power and planning to gain more territory for herself, was neglected. Churchill himself later wrote:

I confess that in my mind the whole Japanese menace lay in a sinister twilight, compared with our other needs.

In fact, he hoped that any attack by Japan would bring the Americans into the war as allies of the British. This indeed happened when on 7 December 1941 the Japanese attacked the American fleet at Pearl Harbour. Churchill's reaction to the news that the Americans were now in the war was simple:

So we had won after all. Hitler's fate was sealed. Mussolini's fate was sealed. As for the Japanese, they would be ground to powder. . .

Fall of Singapore

The immediate results of the war with Japan were disastrous. The Japanese took Singapore in February 1942. Churchill's bodyguard W.H. Thompson later wrote:

His [Churchill's] most anxious period of the war . . . was at the time of the loss of Singapore. He appeared then to be most despondent and deep in thought. When asked by friends what had happened he would look up with sorrow in his face and reply: 'I really do not know. I cannot

understand what has happened'.

Churchill later explained that he had never suspected Singapore's main weakness — lack of fortifications on the landward side (attack had only been expected from the sea):

I ought to have known. My advisers ought to have known and I ought to have been told, and I ought to have asked. The reason I had not asked about this matter, amid the thousands of questions I put, was that the possibility of Singapore having no landward defences no more entered into my mind than that of a battleship being launched without a bottom.

Criticism at home

When another disaster — the German capture of Tobruk in North Africa — followed in June 1942, Churchill had to face criticism in the House of Commons. Sir John Wardlow-Milne proposed the motion:

That this House, while paying tribute to the heroism and endurance of the Armed Forces of the Crown in circumstances of exceptional difficulty, has no confidence in the central direction of the War.

Churchill, it was suggested, should not be in over-all charge of military affairs. Recent defeats were stressed, especially in a witty speech by Hore-Belisha which Churchill himself later quoted in his own history of the war:

We may lose Egypt or we may not lose Egypt — I pray God we may not — but when the Prime Minister, who said that we would hold Singapore, that we would hold Crete, that we had smashed the German army (in North Africa) . . . when I read that he had said that we are going to hold Egypt, my anxieties became greater . . . . How can one place reliance in judgments that have so repeatedly turned out to be misguided?

Again Churchill won the vote of confidence

47

— by 475 to 25. But the Welsh MP Aneurin Bevan had scored a telling point against him:

> . . . the Prime Minister wins debate after debate and loses battle after battle.

From Germany, Goebbels complained that Churchill's "blood, sweat, toil and tears" promise had made him

> totally immune from attack. He is like a doctor who prophesies that his patient will die and who, every time the patient's condition worsens, smugly explains that, after all, he prophesied it.

Churchill himself felt that he badly needed to be able to report a victory.

The Dieppe Raid and the "Second Front"

Instead, there was another set-back in August when a British and Canadian landing at Dieppe in France led only to heavy casualties. This at least helped Churchill to convince the Russians and Americans that it was not possible to start a "second front" by invading Western Europe. In Britain, some people felt that it was a betrayal of Russia not to try, at least, to land forces in Europe. Aneurin Bevan expressed this feeling in the House of Commons:

> . . . we have to do it. We cannot postpone it until next year. Stalin expects it; please do not misunderstand me, for Heaven's sake do not let us make the mistake of betraying those lion-hearted Russians. Speeches have been made, the Russians believe them and have broken the champagne bottles on them . . .

In August 1942 Churchill himself went to Moscow to break the news to Stalin that there was no chance of a "second front" that year. Stalin told him, Churchill recorded, that:

> A man who was not prepared to take risks could not win a war. Why were we so afraid of the Germans? . . . He felt that if the British Army had been fighting the Germans as much as the Russian Army it would not be so frightened of them . . .

Churchill replied that he

> pardoned the remarks which Stalin had made on account of the bravery of the Russian Army.

After a number of meetings, Stalin reluctantly accepted the delay of the "second

32 Churchill and Stalin (separated by the American Averell Harriman) in Moscow in August 1942.

front'' — at least until 1943.

Victory in North Africa

Success came at last in North Africa. In 1941 Churchill had dismissed General Wavell, the Commander-in-Chief in the Middle East, and replaced him with General Auchinleck. This was after Wavell had lost a battle which he had not thought it wise to fight with forces reduced by the failures in Greece and Crete. General Dill, Chief of the Imperial General Staff, explained:

> The fault was not Wavell's, except in so far as he did not resist pressure from Whitehall with sufficient vigour.

And an American soldier, General Raymond E. Lee, who was in London at the time wrote:

> ... I had to admit that I was [shocked], for Wavell is the only British general who has had anything approaching success, in spite of the fact that he has had to make all his 'bricks without straw''.

In 1942 Wavell's successor, General Auchinleck, was also replaced — again, many people thought, unfairly. The new Commander-in-Chief was General Alexander. He and General Montgomery, who was in charge

of the Eighth Army, as the British troops in Egypt were called, refused to attack the Germans who had advanced well into Egypt, until they were ready. Then, on 4 November 1942, Alexander was able to report:

> After twelve days of heavy and violent fighting the Eighth Army has inflicted a severe defeat on the German and Italian forces ...

Churchill commented on this victory in the Battle of El Alamein, in a speech on 10 November:

> ... this is not the end. It is not even the beginning of the end. But it is, perhaps, the end of the beginning.

He remained unrepentant over what other people saw as his constant badgering of his generals. He told Robert Boothby in 1948:

> They say I interfered during the war. I did. I interfered all the time.

The "Big Three"

Britain now had to co-operate with two larger powers, the USA and Russia. Churchill felt

49

that his meetings with Stalin in 1942 had in the end led them "on to easy and friendly terms". As he later wrote,

> Stalin has a very captivating manner when he chooses to use it.

With President Roosevelt, Churchill had a much closer relationship and the two men met frequently. Mrs Roosevelt later recalled:

> It always took him [Franklin Roosevelt] several days to catch up on sleep after Churchill left.

The Casablanca Conference

In January 1943 Churchill met Roosevelt at Casablanca in Morocco — a part of North Africa recently captured by American troops. Harold Macmillan was there too and described the atmosphere of the conference: the two leaders

> were officially called Air Commodore Frankland, who lived in Villa 3, and Admiral Q, who lived in Villa 2 . . . . I christened the two personalities the Emperor of the East and the Emperor of the West, and indeed it was rather like a meeting of the later period of the Roman Empire . . .

A controversial decision made at Casablanca was to demand unconditional surrender (that is, surrender without advance offers of peace terms) from Germany, Italy and Japan. The danger was that this would make the enemy resist longer — but in fact, Churchill very soon explained that "unconditional surrender" did not mean brutal treatment of defeated enemies. He told the House of Commons on 22 February 1944:

> Unconditional surrender means that the victors have a free hand. It does not mean that they are entitled to behave in a barbarous manner, nor that they wish to blot out Germany from among the nations of Europe . . .

The Tehran Conference

It was again necessary to explain to Stalin that "Operation Overlord" — the attack on France which had been under discussion since 1942 — was to be postponed. It had been decided in Casablanca to invade Sicily, not France, in 1943. Even when planning for 1944, Churchill was determined not to act in haste. He wrote to Eden, who visited Moscow in October 1943, asking him to make Britain's position clear to Stalin:

> 26 October 1943
>
> You should let him know . . . that I will not allow . . . the great and fruitful campaign in Italy . . . to be cast away and end in a frightful disaster, for the sake of crossing the Channel in May . . . . We will do our very best for 'Overlord', but it is no use planning for defeat in the field in order to give temporary political satisfaction.

In November 1943 Stalin met Roosevelt and Churchill at the Tehran Conference. He was deeply suspicious:

> I wish to pose a very direct question to the Prime Minister about 'Overlord'. Do the Prime Minister and the British Staff [officers] really believe in 'Overlord'?

Churchill replied:

> Provided the conditions previously stated for 'Overlord' are established when the time comes, it will be our stern duty to hurl across the Channel against the Germans every sinew of our strength.

The Tehran Conference ended with Churchill's birthday dinner on 30 November. He later wrote:

> This was a memorable occasion in my life. On my right sat the President of the United States, on my left the Master of Russia . . . . I could not help rejoicing at the long way we had come on the road to victory since the summer of 1940 . . .

Chapter Nine 1944-1945
Victory and Defeat

"Operation Overlord" was very thoroughly prepared. The date of D Day, the day when landings in France would be made, was finally fixed for early June 1944. Churchill wanted to be there when the troops landed in Normandy — or at least to watch from a British ship. In his history of the war he recalled:

> Eisenhower [then Supreme Commander of the invasion of Europe] protested against my running such risks. As Supreme Commander he could not bear the responsibility. I sent him word . . . that . . . we did not in any way admit his right to regulate the complements [men on board] of the British ships . . . . He accepted this undoubted fact, but dwelt on the addition this would impose upon his anxieties. This appeared to be out of proportion . . . . I too had responsibilities, and felt I must be my own judge of my movements. The matter was settled accordingly.

After much persuasion, King George VI succeeded where Eisenhower had failed. He wrote:

> Buckingham Palace
> June 2, 1944
>
> My dear Winston,
>   I want to make one more appeal to you not to go to sea on D Day . . . . There is

nothing I would like better than to go to sea, but I have agreed to stay at home; is it fair that you should then do exactly what I should have liked to do myself? . . .

Churchill's reply was:

> June 3, 1944
>
> Sir
>   . . . Since your Majesty does me the honour to be so much concerned about my personal safety on this occasion, I must defer to Your Majesty's wishes, and indeed commands . . .
>   Your Majesty's humble and devoted
>   servant and subject,
>   Winston S. Churchill

It was a most reluctant decision. Churchill later commented:

> A man who has to play an effective part in taking . . . grave and terrible decisions of war may need the refreshment of adventure. He may need also the comfort that when sending so many others to their deaths he may share in a small way their risks.

D Day, 6 June 1944

Instead, on 6 June 1944 at noon, Churchill was in the House of Commons, making an important statement:

> I have also to announce to the House

34 Churchill was at last able to visit British troops in France on 12 June 1944, a week after D Day. Montgomery (left) prepares to welcome him.

that during the night and the early hours of this morning the first of the series of landings in force upon the European continent has taken place . . . so far the commanders . . . report that every thing is proceeding according to plan. And what a plan! this vast operation is undoubtedly the most complicated and difficult that has ever taken place . . .

Visit to France

Churchill himself was in France a few days later. He wrote:

On June 10 General Montgomery reported that he was sufficiently established ashore to receive a visit . . . . The weather was brilliant. We drove through our limited but fertile domain in Normandy . . . . The inhabitants seemed quite buoyant and well-nourished and waved enthusiastically . . .

General de Gaulle

Just before D Day, Churchill had had one of many quarrels with Charles de Gaulle, the leader of the Free French (Frenchmen who had escaped to Britain to continue the fight). He described de Gaulle as "that most difficult man". The general was already "bristling" over being informed very late about the invasion plans, when Churchill further offended him by remarking:

If there was a split between . . . [de Gaulle] and the United States we should most certainly side with the Americans . . . .

Churchill recorded:

I had expected that de Gaulle would dine with us and come back to London . . . but he drew himself up and stated that he preferred to motor . . . separately.

Churchill later wrote about de Gaulle:

I understood and admired, while I resented, his arrogant demeanour . . . . The Germans had conquered his country. He had no real foothold anywhere. Never mind; he defied all. Always, even when he was behaving worst, he seemed to express the personality of France — a great nation, with all its pride, authority and ambition.

Now in the autumn of 1944, Churchill helped to persuade the Americans to recognize de Gaulle as head of the new French government. In November, a visit to liberated Paris was a great success. Churchill wrote to Roosevelt:

I certainly had a wonderful reception from about half a million French in the Champs Elysées . . . . I re-established friendly private relations with de Gaulle.

Visit to Italy

More "refreshment of adventure" came from a visit to the Italian front in August 1944. Churchill was particularly pleased by General Alexander's promise

to take me wherever I wanted to go . . . this was the nearest I got to the enemy and the time I heard most bullets in the second World War.

Alexander later gave his own account:

Winston was always bothering me to take him up to the front to see a battle . . . now he was more insistent than ever, and I thought, well, after all, we have practically won the war at last. So, when we were advancing, I took him in a jeep close behind the assault troops . . . .

We could hear the machine-guns of the infantry going rat-tat-tat-tat just below us, and on the hill in front . . . our tanks were creeping up . . . . Winston saw it all like a demonstration, and was as happy as the

proverbial sand-boy.

War-weariness

No one knew how long the war might still last. A new menace appeared in the summer of 1944; during July and August Churchill's memos were full of references to "the robots" — the flying-bombs directed at London. In September rockets began to land, though fortunately most of their launching sites were soon captured. Churchill had been seriously ill with pneumonia at the end of 1943. Even he was now suffering from the long strain. This made him more difficult than ever to work for. "Pug" Ismay, Churchill's Chief of Staff, described in a letter Churchill's bad-temper on a voyage to Canada to discuss important future plans with the Americans:

15 September 1944
Master has been extraordinarily difficult — so much so that . . . I wrote yesterday offering to resign. He dealt with it in typical fashion; handed it back to me saying: 'don't write me this sort of rubbish, dear Pug: we are going to the end — together — you and I. I'm sorry if I get angry, but you must admit I have cause.' I replied that he had abundant cause, but why vent it all on me! and why give me the feeling that I could do nothing right. He denied this: said he had every confidence in me, and was much dependent on my industry, tact and judgment . . .

Visit to Moscow

Churchill was already worried about what was to happen to Europe when the war ended. Russia and the USA were both now much stronger than Britain. On a visit to Moscow in October 1944, he tried to strike a bargain with Stalin, and recorded this later in his history of the war:

The moment was apt for business, so I said, "Let us settle about our affairs in the Balkans . . .". I wrote out on a half-sheet of paper:

Roumania	
Russia	90%
The others	10%
Greece	
Great Britain	90%
(in accord with U.S.A.)	
Russia	10%
Yugoslavia	50-50%
Hungary	50-50%
Bulgaria	
Russia	75%
The others	25%

I pushed this to Stalin . . . . There was a slight pause. Then he took his blue pencil and made a large tick upon it . . .

The figures showed the amount of influence the Great Powers were to have over the smaller states.

Intervention in Greece

Britain was determined to keep her influence in Greece. Greek Communist Resistance groups tried at the end of 1944 to seize power there when the Germans were driven

35 Churchill, Roosevelt and Stalin at Yalta, February 1945. President Roosevelt looks tired and ill. He died on 12 April 1945.

out. Churchill told the British commander that the Communist attempt to take power must be put down:

> We have to hold and dominate Athens. It would be a great thing for you to succeed in this without bloodshed if possible, but also with bloodshed if necessary.

Churchill himself later recorded the fierce criticism of his action:

> The vast majority of the American Press violently condemned our action, which they declared falsified the cause for which they had gone to war . . . . The *Times* and the *Manchester Guardian* pronounced their censures . . . . Stalin however adhered strictly . . . to our agreement of October, and during all the long weeks of fighting the Communists in the streets of Athens not one word of reproach came from

Pravda or *Isvestia* [the Russian newspapers]. In the House of Commons there was a great stir . . .

Churchill made his defence:

> I say that the last thing that represents democracy is mob law . . . . Do not let us rate democracy so low, do not let us rate democracy as if it were merely grabbing power and shooting those who do not agree with you . . .

The House of Commons voted in support of Churchill's action by 281 to 32, but many members abstained. Eventually Churchill visited Athens and took part in discussion which led in January 1945 to a compromise settlement and a truce.

The Yalta Conference

In February 1945 Stalin, Roosevelt and Churchill met for the last time, at Yalta, in Russia. The Americans wanted Russia to enter the war against Japan and, in return, were ready to give Stalin what he wanted in Europe. The agreement made between Churchill and Stalin in Moscow in 1944 was confirmed. Russia was to control Roumania and Bulgaria. In addition, Churchill had

reluctantly to agree to a Russian-influenced government in Poland. In the House of Commons his report on Yalta was, or tried to be, optimistic:

> The . . . Conference leaves the Allies more closely united than before . . . . Most solemn declarations have been made by Marshal Stalin that the sovereign independence of Poland is to be maintained . . .

At a later date, he could only plead necessity:

> It is easy, after the Germans are beaten, to condemn those who did their best to hearten the Russian military effort and to keep in harmonious contact with our great Ally who had suffered so frightfully. What would have happened if we had quarrelled with Russia while the Germans still had two or three hundred divisions on the fighting front?

But his critics were not silenced. Robert Boothby later wrote a scathing attack on the Yalta agreements:

> At Yalta whole nations had been handed around like plums, without any regard

36   Londoners surround Churchill on VE Day.

to their own wishes. 'Allright, old boy', they said, over the caviar, vodka and cigars, 'We'll give you Bulgaria and Roumania if you give us Greece'.

The bombing of Germany

More criticism arose from the continued heavy bombing of German cities, when the end of the war seemed in sight. The bomb attack on Dresden in February 1945 killed over 60,000 people. Churchill had not directly ordered this attack, but he approved of the general policy. In his own history of the war, he referred to the bombing of Dresden only as "a heavy raid" on "a centre of communications". In April 1945, however, he pressed successfully for an end to bombing, pointing out the disadvantage to the Allies of taking over "an entirely ruined land".

The death of Roosevelt

Early on 13 April 1945 Churchill was told of the death of the American President. He later wrote:

When I received these tidings . . . I felt as if I had been struck a physical blow . . .

At the time, in a letter to an American friend, he said simply:

I had a true affection for Franklin.

Victory in Europe

The war with Germany ended on 8 May 1945. Surrounded by cheering crowds of Londoners, Churchill made one of his shortest speeches from a balcony in Whitehall:

God bless you all. This is your victory! It is the victory of the cause of freedom in every land. In all our long history we have never seen a greater day than this. Everyone, man or woman, has done their best. Everyone has tried. Neither the long years, nor the dangers, nor the fierce attacks of the enemy, have in any way weakened the independent resolve of the British nation. God bless you all.

37 Churchill agreed with the American decision to ▷ use the atom bomb against Japan. This explosion took place at Hiroshima on 6 August 1945.

A General Election

At Yalta in February 1945 Churchill had told Stalin that

there would be a General Election in the United Kingdom after the defeat of Hitler. Stalin thought my position was assured, "since the people would understand that they needed a leader, and who could be a better leader than he who had won the victory?" I explained that we had two parties in Britain, and I only belonged to one of them. "One party is much better," said Stalin, with deep conviction.

The election date was 5 July. Although Churchill would have preferred to continue the national government, once the campaign started he fought hard. He shocked many people by a broadcast in which he proclaimed:

No Socialist system can be established without a political police . . . . They would have to fall back on some form of Gestapo, no doubt very humanely directed in the first instance . . .

This seemed to be the old Churchill — the "wild man" — back again.

Harold Macmillan later described the atmosphere of the campaign:

Churchill was buoyed up by the enthusiastic reception which he received in his thousand-mile electoral tour. Vast crowds . . . turned out in flocks to see and applaud him. They wished to thank him for what he had done for them; and in that all were sincere. But this did not mean that they wished to entrust him and his Tory colleagues with the conduct of their lives in the years that were to follow . . .

The result of the election was not known for three weeks, because the soldiers' votes

had to be collected in. People remembered the unemployment of the 1930s, wanted drastic reforms and voted Labour.

A Labour victory

Labour's victory was announced on 26 July. Churchill later wrote that:

> . . . the verdict of the electors had been so overwhelmingly expressed that I did not wish to remain even for an hour responsible for their affairs.

He resigned as Prime Minister that evening. Macmillan, who lost his own seat, remembered how, on the following day Churchill seemed still somewhat dazed by the blow, but not a word of recrimination escaped him:

> I felt that he owed no apology to the party. It was not he who had dragged us down. It was we who had somehow hoped to get through by clinging to his coat-tails.

Naturally, Churchill felt bitter. On a holiday in Italy he told General Alexander:

> You know, when I was turned out of office, I felt it to be a very hard thing after all I had done.

Again, as he had done after Gallipoli and in the 1930s, Churchill turned to painting and writing.

The Atom bomb

One of Churchill's first major speeches as Leader of the Opposition was made in support of the decision that the Americans should use the atom bomb against Japan. This decision had been made while he was still Prime Minister, although the bombs were not dropped until August. Japan surrendered on 14 August. On 16 August Churchill told the House of Commons:

> There are voices which assert that the bomb should never have been used at all. I cannot associate myself with such ideas. Six years of total war have convinced most people that had the Germans or Japanese discovered this new weapon, they would have used it upon us to our complete destruction with the utmost alacrity.

In his account of the end of the war, published in 1954, Churchill still stood by this decision:

> To quell the Japanese resistance man by man and conquer the country yard by yard might well require the loss of a million American lives and half that number of British . . . .
> British consent in principle to the use of the weapon had been given on July 4 . . . . The final decision now lay in the main with President Truman . . . but I never doubted what it would be, nor have I ever doubted since that he was right.

Chapter Ten 1945-1965

Elder Statesman

Churchill travelled widely while the Conservatives were in opposition. He was honoured by governments, and he was also admired by ordinary people. Robert Boothby visited a French café with him in 1948:

> The bill was then demanded. Unthinkable, said the proprietress. It was the greatest honour they had ever had. Perhaps Monsieur Churchill would sign his name in the book? Monsieur Churchill would; and did. I went out . . . wondering whether I would ever be famous enough to pay bills with my signature.

The "Iron Curtain"

On a visit to the United States in 1946 Churchill made a speech at Fulton, Missouri, in which he stressed the possible danger from Russia. He used publicly a term he had earlier used in writing to President Truman — the "iron curtain":

> From Stettin in the Baltic to Trieste in the Adriatic an iron curtain has descended across the continent.

Harold Macmillan later described American reaction to Churchill's speech:

> . . . he shook and even shocked American opinion . . . . What was the old statesman doing? Was it restlessness? Was it disappointment over his loss of office? Or — unpleasant thought — could he perhaps

be right? After all, he had been right before.

A United Europe

One of Churchill's post-war interests was the movement for European unity. Early in 1947 he helped to found the United Europe Movement and in 1949 he was one of the Conservative representatives at the first meeting of the new Assembly of Europe at Strasbourg. There, said Macmillan, he sat

> between two Italians with whom he conversed volubly and audibly in his characteristic French.

As usual he was eager for a reconciliation with old enemies — now safely defeated. He asked "Where are the Germans?" and pressed for them to be invited at once to join. West Germany was invited the following year.

Just after leaving Strasbourg, Churchill had the first of a series of strokes. Macmillan reported that the stroke "by careful control of the news was effectively concealed". It was important to the Conservatives that their leader should not appear unfit.

The "war-monger" again

Churchill's warnings concerning Russia brought accusations of war-mongering from his opponents in Britain, especially near and at parliamentary election time. In May 1951 the Labour minister Dalton announced:

38 Churchill was honoured throughout post-war Europe. Here he and his wife (far left) visit the Dutch royal family in 1948.

If we get Churchill and the Tory Party back at the next election we shall be at war with Russia within twelve months.

In his own election speeches in October that year, Churchill took care to deny that he wanted or expected war.

If I remain in public life . . . it is because . . . I believe I may be able to make an important contribution to the prevention of a third world war . . . . It is the last prize I seek to win.

Electioneering

Although he was now 77, Churchill still relished the excitement of an election campaign. The Chairman of his constituency Conservative Association wrote in 1953:

No candidate anywhere in the country enjoys his election meetings more than Churchill . . . . Just before Polling Day Churchill tours the district in an open car . . . our schedules are invariably dis-

organised by the candidate himself as his mounting and infectious enthusiasm leads him to make many more stops and many more speeches than we plan . . .

Prime Minister again

The Conservatives won the October 1951 election with a small majority. Churchill was delighted to be back in office as Prime Minister. Harold Macmillan was made Minister of Housing, and his description of his interview with Churchill shows well both the Prime Minister's genuine concern for "the people" and his lack of real knowledge of domestic affairs. He asked Macmillan to

'build the houses for the people' . . . I asked what was the present housing 'set up'. He said he had not an idea, but the 'boys' [i.e. the civil servants] would know.

There was some anxiety, even amongst Conservatives, about Churchill's age and health. Montgomery later bluntly told Robert Boothby:

Winston should never have become Prime Minister in 1951; he was an old and tired man.

39 "Dropping the pilot" had been a famous cartoon ▷
recording the dismissal of the great German statesman
Bismarck. Here the cartoonist reverses the idea:
Churchill in 1951 wins the election and John Bull
calls him "aboard" again, as Prime Minister.

A new reign

Churchill was still Prime Minister two years
later when a new ruler, Queen Elizabeth II
was crowned. He was made a Knight of the
Garter, so that he was now "Sir Winston",
and greatly enjoyed wearing the splendid
robes. At the Coronation in June Harold
Nicolson saw him "waving his plumed hat
and making the V sign" to the crowds.
However, he was soon ill again, and though
he continued to work, especially for a new
meeting of world leaders, his colleagues tried
to persuade him to retire. In April 1955

THE PILOT GOES ABOARD AGAIN

they were successful — and then, as Macmillan
wrote:

> Now that he has really decided to go, we
> are all miserable.

The *Times* reported on his departure from 10
Downing Street on 6 April 1955:

> Smoking a cigar, and greeting the crowd

◁ 40 The cover of *The Washington Daily News* for 5
April 1955 — the day of Churchill's resignation as
Prime Minister of Great Britain. No words were
needed — everyone would recognise the "V" sign.

gathered in Downing Street with his famous V sign, Sir Winston Churchill drove slowly away to the accompaniment of cheers and shouts of good wishes.

Last years

Churchill's last years were sad. He could not be active now and was often depressed. However, he enjoyed the fuss made of him on special occasions, especially on his birthdays. He died on 24 January 1965. The Queen ordered that he should be given a state funeral, with a magnificent procession and a service in St Paul's Cathedral. He was then buried with other members of the family of the Dukes of Marlborough at Bladon in Oxfordshire.

The summing-up

More than 320,000 ordinary people filed past Churchill's coffin when his body lay in state before the funeral. They had come to pay their respects to someone who had been, as the *Times* said, "The great war leader of his age". Twenty years earlier, one of the best comments on Churchill and his controversial career had been made by a political opponent, Emmanuel Shinwell:

I do my best to dislike Churchill; there is abundant reason why I should . . . . But he has served his country with the highest distinction . . . how can one work up an intense dislike for a man who has 'borne the heat and burden of the day . . .'?

The historian A.J.P. Taylor put it even more simply. In his history of the period 1914-1945, published in 1965, he ended his brief biography of Churchill with the words: "The saviour of his country". Churchill, who loved praise, would not have asked for more.

Date List

Early life

1874	30 November	Winston Leonard Spencer Churchill is born at Blenheim Palace, home of his grandfather, the Duke of Marlborough.
1888-92		Schooldays at Harrow. Churchill never does justice to his ability at school.
1893		He enters Sandhurst for military training.
1895		Death of Lord Randolph Churchill, Winston's father. Churchill joins the army (4th Hussars). Starts writing career, selling articles to *Daily Graphic*.
1897		Churchill in India, serving in the army.
1898	March	Churchill's first book *The Malakand Field Force* published.
	August	In Egypt with the army.
	2 September	Churchill takes part in Battle of Omdurman.

42 Winston Churchill aged 12.

The Junior Member for Oldham

1899		Churchill resigns from army to enter politics.
	6 July	He is defeated as Conservative candidate for Oldham.
	October	Boer War breaks out in South Africa. Churchill goes out as reporter for the *Morning Post.*
	15 November	Churchill captured by Boers.
	12 December	He escapes.
1900	March	Churchill takes part in the relief of Ladysmith. He returns to England as a hero.
	1 October	Churchill wins the election at Oldham.
1901	February	Churchill makes his maiden speech (his first speech in the House of Commons).

	May	Britain makes peace with the Boers (Peace of Vereeniging).
1903		Some Conservatives, led by Joseph Chamberlain, press for Tariff Reform. Churchill supports Free Trade.
1904		Churchill finally leaves the Conservative party.
	May	He joins the Liberals.
1905	December	Conservative government defeated in House of Commons. Liberals form a government and offer Churchill post of Under Secretary for the Colonies.
1906	January	Election. Churchill stands as Liberal candidate for North West Manchester and wins seat. Liberals win election.

The Liberal Minister

		Churchill publishes a biography of his father (*Lord Randolph Churchill*).
1907		As Under Secretary for the Colonies, Churchill visits East Africa.
1908	April	Asquith, the new Prime Minister, appoints Churchill as President of the Board of Trade. He is now in the Cabinet, and has to be re-elected as MP. He loses at Manchester, but soon wins another seat at Dundee.
	12 September	Churchill marries Clementine Hozier.
1909		Churchill supports Lloyd George, the Chancellor of the Exchequer, in resisting heavy spending on defence, including the Navy. He supports the "People's Budget" against the House of Lords, making speeches throughout the country.
	July	The Churchills' first child, Diana, is born.
	September	Parliament passes the Labour Exchange Act, carrying out Churchill's plan to establish Labour Exchanges to make it easier for people to find jobs.
1910	January	Election. Churchill keeps his seat at Dundee. The Liberals retain power (with Labour and Irish support) and introduce a Parliament Bill to reduce the power of the House of Lords.
	14 February	Churchill is promoted to the post of Home Secretary.
	November	Riots at Tonypandy. Churchill sends extra police, with soldiers in reserve. He is criticized by Right and Left.
	December	Election. Liberals retain power. Churchill is re-elected at Dundee.
1911	3 January	Churchill goes to Sidney Street to watch a struggle between police and gunmen.
		Churchill supports Lloyd George in introducing a National Insurance Bill.
	May	The Churchills' son Randolph is born.
	August	House of Lords passes the Parliament Bill. Churchill is criticized for over-reacting in his use of troops to prevent disturbances during Railway Strike.

At the Admiralty

1911	September	Churchill is offered the post of First Lord of the Admiralty.
1912	February	The Churchills visit Belfast. Churchill speaks to the Ulster

		Liberal Association.
		Irish Home Rule bill is introduced. Churchill supports it in House of Commons. It is passed, but House of Lords delays it until 1914.
		Churchill takes his first flight in an aeroplane.
		In the face of German naval expansion, he urges on the building of British battleships.
1913-14		Churchill quarrels with Lloyd George over the Navy Estimates. He obtains more money for battleships.
1914	March	Churchill is criticized for his readiness to send warships to overawe Ulster when Ulster prepares to resist Home Rule.
	4 August	War with Germany. Churchill has the British Fleet already in position at Scapa Flow.
		Home Rule for Ireland is postponed until after the war.
	October	Churchill goes to Antwerp, Belgium, to rally resistance. He insists that Admiral Fisher is re-appointed First Sea Lord.
	Winter	In Western Europe a long period of trench warfare begins.
1915	January	Churchill convinces War Council that an expedition to seize the Dardanelles will shorten the war.
	March	Naval attack on the Dardanelles fails.
	April	Military expedition to the Gallipoli peninsula meets with little success.
	May	Fisher resigns amid mounting criticism of the Dardanelles campaign.
		Churchill is removed from the Admiralty. He accepts minor government post (Chancellor of the Duchy of Lancaster) in Asquith's coalition government.
	November	Churchill is not included in the new Cabinet War Committee. He resigns from the government, which soon decides to withdraw from Gallipoli.

Coalition

1915	18 November	Churchill leaves England to join the army fighting in France.
	December	He goes as Commanding Officer to the 6th Battalion Royal Scots Fusiliers.
1916	7 March	Churchill, on leave, makes a rash speech in the House of Commons, suggesting Fisher should return as First Sea Lord.
	May	He leaves the army to return to political life.
	December	Lloyd George replaces Asquith as Prime Minister. Churchill

		is bitterly disappointed not to be given a post in the government.
1917	July	Churchill returns to office as Minister of Munitions, but he is still not in the Cabinet.
1918	11 November	Crowds cheer the Churchills on Armistice Day, when war with Germany ends.
1919	10 January	Churchill becomes Secretary for War and Air. He supports intervention in Russia (giving aid to White Russians against Bolsheviks).
	November	Churchill back in the Cabinet.
1920		Churchill favours a hard line against the IRA in Ireland.
1921	February	Churchill is made Colonial Secretary.
	March	He attends Cairo Conference to settle the future of an independent Iraq, and visits Palestine.
	May	Churchill supports in Cabinet a policy of concessions and truce in Ireland. (A truce was achieved in July.)
	December	The Irish Treaty is signed, giving Southern Ireland (now the Irish Free State) self-government.
1922		Churchill buys Chartwell Manor, Kent which becomes his country home.
	September	Although now drifting away from the Liberals, Churchill supports Lloyd George's firm stand when Turkey threatens the British base at Chanak. War seems close but is avoided.
	19 October	The Conservatives decide to leave the Coalition government; Lloyd George resigns as Prime Minister.
	15 November	Election. Many Liberals, including Churchill, lose their seats.

The Conservative Chancellor

1923		Churchill publishes volume 1 of *The World Crisis,* his study of the 1914-18 war.
	December	Election. Churchill fails to win a seat.
1924	January	The first Labour government comes into office with Liberal support.

44 Chartwell Manor, Kent — Churchill's country house.

	March	Churchill loses by 43 votes at the Westminster by-election.
	September	He is chosen as a candidate by Epping Conservatives.
	October	Election. Churchill wins Epping and returns to the House of Commons. The Conservatives win the election.
	November	The Prime Minister, Baldwin, appoints Churchill as Chancellor of the Exchequer.
1925	January	Churchill opposes high spending on the Navy because he wants to reduce taxation.
	28 April	Churchill introduces the first of his annual budgets, cutting income tax by 6d (2½p) to 4/- (20p) in the pound, and raising pensions. He also announces Britain's return to the "Gold Standard" in May.
1926	3-12 May	General Strike. Churchill edits the *British Gazette* and is blamed for its unfairness to the strikers.
	August-September	Churchill tries, but fails, to negotiate good terms for the miners who stay on strike.
1928	April	Budget. In order to encourage industrial expansion and reduce unemployment, Churchill's budget reduces the rates which industries have to pay.
1929	May	Election. The Conservatives lose. Churchill wins at Epping but is out of office for the next ten years.

In the Wilderness

		Labour party again forms a government.
1930		Churchill's autobiography, *My Early Life*, is published. He opposes the policy of dominion status for India, which Baldwin, leader of the Conservative Party, is ready to accept.
1931	January	Churchill resigns from the Conservative "Shadow Cabinet".
	August	Economic crisis. The Labour Prime Minister Ramsay Macdonald forms a National government of members of all parties. Churchill is not included.
1933	January	Hitler comes to power in Germany.
	March	Churchill warns against German rearmament and refers to the "most grim dictatorship" there.
	October	Churchill publishes the first volume of his biography, *Marlborough*.
1935	June	Baldwin again Prime Minister. Does not include Churchill in his government.
1936	March	Hitler reoccupies the Rhineland.
		Churchill continues to warn against Germany's ambition.
	December	Edward VIII abdicates. Churchill tries without success to prevent this.
1937	May	Neville Chamberlain succeeds Baldwin as Prime Minister.
1938	March	Hitler takes over Austria.
	September	Crisis over German claims to territory belonging to Czechoslovakia.
	29/30 September	Munich Agreement gives Germany the Sudetenland. Churchill criticizes this settlement in the House of Commons.

45 Caught off duty waiting for a train at Oxford in 1941, Churchill looks older and grimmer than in his posed photographs.

1939	March	Hitler occupies the rest of Czechoslovakia.
		Churchill urges cooperation with Russia against Germany.
	1 September	Hitler attacks Poland.

The War Leader — Saving Britain

1939	3 September	Britain declares war on Germany. Churchill returns to the Admiralty as First Lord.
1940	April	British expedition to Norway sets out. It fails in May.
	7-8 May	Criticism of Chamberlain in House of Commons. 33 Conservatives vote against the government.
	10 May	The Germans invade Holland and Belgium.

Chamberlain resigns and Churchill becomes Prime Minister of a National Government. He is also Minister of Defence.

	3-4 June	Successful evacuation of British troops from Dunkirk completed.
	4 June	Churchill makes his "fight on the beaches" speech: "we shall never surrender".
	11 June	Italy (under her Dictator Mussolini) enters the war on Germany's side.
	22 June	France surrenders to Germany.
	3 July	British ships destroy French warships at Oran.

German air attacks on Britain begin.

	13-August- 15 September	The "Battle of Britain" is fought in the air. In September, the "Blitz" on London begins.
	17 September	Hitler postpones any invasion of Britain.
	October	Churchill succeeds Neville Chamberlain as Leader of the Conservative party.

The War Leader — Fighting a World War

1941	11 March	The American Congress passes the Lend-Lease Bill, confirming that in exchange for leasing bases to the USA, the British can buy war materials on credit.
	April	Evacuation of British troops sent to help Greece.
	7 May	Churchill faces criticism in the House of Commons but wins a vote of confidence 447-3.
	27 May	British withdrawal from Crete.
	15-17 June	Unsuccessful offensive by Commander-in-Chief Wavell in North Africa. He is replaced.

	22 June	Germans invade Russia. Churchill welcomes Russia as an ally.
	August	Churchill meets Roosevelt on board ship. They issue a joint statement of ideals — the "Atlantic Charter".
	7 December	Churchill hears of the Japanese attack early that day on Pearl Harbour. Britain declares war on Japan and the United States now joins the war against Germany.
	26 December	While visiting Roosevelt at the White House in Washington, Churchill speaks to the American Congress. He suffers a slight heart attack during this American visit.
1942	15 January	Churchill flies back to England.
	27-29 January	Another "vote of confidence" debate in the House of Commons. Churchill wins 464-1.
	15 February	Singapore surrenders to the Japanese.
	21 June	On a visit to Washington, Churchill hears of the fall of Tobruk in North Africa to the Germans.
	1-2 July	House of Commons debate on the conduct of the war. Churchill wins a "vote of confidence" 475-25.
	August	Churchill visits the Eighth Army in Egypt. He decides to put General Alexander in command in North Africa. He flies on to Moscow to meet Stalin.
	23 October	Battle of El Alamein begins.
	8 November	American and British troops land in French North Africa.
1943	January	Churchill and Roosevelt meet in North Africa — the Casablanca Conference.
	12 and 13 May	Germans in North Africa surrender.
	9 July	Allied troops invade Sicily.
	August	Churchill and Roosevelt meet in Quebec.
	September	Italian mainland invaded. Italy surrenders, but Germans continue to fight in Italy.
	November	Churchill, Roosevelt and Stalin meet in Iran — the Tehran Conference.
	December	Churchill seriously ill with pneumonia in North Africa. He has to rest, and goes to Marrakesh in Morocco.
1944	January	Churchill returns to England. Preparations for "Overlord", the invasion of France, are now well underway.

Victory and Defeat

1944	6 June	D Day — the Allies land in France.
	12 June	Churchill visits France.
	13 June	First flying-bomb falls on London.
	August	Churchill visits the Italian front.
	8 September	First rocket falls on London.
	11-16 September	Churchill meets Roosevelt in Quebec.
	9-17 October	Churchill meets Stalin in Moscow.
	December	Churchill is criticized for putting down Greek Communist attempt to take power in Athens.

	24-28 December	Churchill visits Athens and discussions lead to a truce in January 1945.
1945	February	Churchill, Roosevelt and Stalin meet in Russia — the Yalta Conference.
	14 February	The bombing of Dresden highlights the casualties and destruction caused by the Allies' policy of intensive air raids on non-military targets.
	March	Allied armies cross the Rhine.
	12 April	Death of Roosevelt.
	8 May	Churchill announces Victory in Europe (VE) Day. Britain prepares for an election.
	23 May	Churchill resigns, ending the National government. He returns as Prime Minister of a "caretaker government".
	5 July	General election. (Voting takes place on 5 July, but to allow time to collect all the servicemen's votes, the result is not announced until 26 July.)
	17 July	Churchill meets the new American President, Harry S. Truman, and Stalin in Germany — the Potsdam Conference. During a break in this conference he returns to England for the election result.
	26 July	Results of election announced. The Conservatives lose. Attlee forms a Labour government. Churchill, re-elected as MP for Woodford (part of his old Epping constituency now reorganized), becomes Leader of the Opposition.
	August	Churchill supports the American decision to use atom bombs on Japan. The Japanese decide to surrender.
	2 September	V.J. (Victory in Japan) Day marks the end of the war.

Elder Statesman

1946		Churchill makes "Iron Curtain" speech at Fulton, Missouri.
1947		Royal Academy accepts two of Churchill's paintings.
1948	May	Churchill attends conference of "United Europe" campaign at The Hague.
	October	Publishes first volume of *The Second World War*.
1949	August	Attends first Consultative Assembly for Western Europe at Strasbourg. Suffers a slight stroke, but soon recovers.
1951	February	Election. Churchill re-elected for Woodford. Labour wins the election.
	October	Election. Churchill accused of being "warmonger", but Conservatives win election.
	26 October	Churchill Prime Minister again.
1953	5 March	Death of Stalin. Churchill presses for new talks with Russia.
	April	Receives Order of the Garter.
	June	Coronation of Elizabeth II.
	23 June	Churchill has another stroke. He recovers gradually.
	October	Churchill wins Nobel Prize for Literature.

	December	Churchill meets with President Eisenhower in Bermuda. The Americans oppose a summit meeting with the Russians.
1954	30 November	Parliament celebrates Churchill's 80th birthday.
1955	5 April	Churchill resigns as Prime Minister.
	26 May	Election. Churchill is re-elected for Woodford. Conservatives win election.
1956	April	Publishes first volume of *History of the English Speaking Peoples.*
	May	Wins Charlemagne Prize (for contributing to European unity).
1958		Appeal launched to build a "Churchill College" at Cambridge.
1959	October	Election. Churchill re-elected for Woodford. Conservatives win election.
1963	May	The Americans make Churchill an Honorary citizen of the United States.
	27 July	He attends the House of Commons for the last time.
1965	24 January	Death of Churchill.

46 Churchill's funeral procession. On the coffin are his Garter badges and collar. The sailors are a reminder of his years at the Admiralty.

Biographical Notes on Churchill's Contemporaries

Alexander, Harold Rupert Leofric George, General (1891-1969) was the last British officer out of Dunkirk in 1940. Churchill appointed him Commander-in-Chief in the Middle East in 1942 and he drove the Germans out of North Africa. As Supreme Allied Commander in the Mediterranean, he was later responsible for the campaigns in Italy. Unlike some of the British generals, he got on well with Churchill. After the war he served as governor-general of Canada (1946-1952) and as Churchill's Minister of Defence (1952-54). He was created Viscount in 1946 and Earl Alexander of Tunis in 1952.

Asquith, Herbert Henry (1852-1928) was a Liberal politician who was Chancellor of the Exchequer 1905-08 and then Prime Minister 1908-16. His later quarrels with Lloyd George split the Liberal party. He was created Earl of Oxford in 1925.

Attlee, Clement (1883-1967) became leader of the Labour party in 1935. He refused to serve under Chamberlain in 1940 but agreed to join Churchill's War Cabinet. From 1942 to 1945 he was Deputy Prime Minister. When Labour won the 1945 election, Attlee succeeded Churchill as Prime Minister (1945-1951). He was created Earl Attlee in 1955.

Auchinleck, Claude John Eyre, General (1884-   ) was transferred from the post of Commander-in-Chief in India in July 1941, to take over Wavell's command in the Middle East. There, in August 1942, Auchinleck himself was replaced, by Churchill, with General Alexander, although he had begun to rebuild the Eighth Army after its defeat by the Germans. Auchinleck returned to India as Commander-in-Chief in June 1943. In 1946 he was promoted to Field Marshal.

Baldwin, Stanley (1867-1947) was a Conservative politician who served as Chancellor of the Exchequer (1922-23) and as Prime Minister 1923-24, 1924-29, 1935-37. He recognized Churchill's great ability and, despite disagreements in the 1930s, they remained friends. Baldwin was created Earl Baldwin in 1937.

Balfour, Arthur James (1848-1930) was Conservative Prime Minister (1902-05) when Churchill was a young Conservative MP. Later he succeeded Churchill as First Lord of the Admiralty (1915-16) and also served as Foreign Secretary (1916-19) and Lord President of the Council (1919-22, 1925-29). Balfour had a reputation for making clever speeches and witty remarks. He was created Earl in 1922.

Beaverbrook, Lord (1879-1964) was born in Canada. As Max Aitken, he made his fortune

47 Lord Curzon, as Foreign Secretary, found Churchill all too ready to offer unwanted advice.

in business, then came to England and went into Parliament as a Conservative. From 1919 he owned the *Daily Express* and used it to put forward his political views. He was, at times, a close friend of Churchill (they often quarrelled) and served as Minister of Aircraft Production and Minister of Supply 1940-42.

Bevan, Aneurin (1897-1960) was a Welsh miner who entered the House of Commons in 1929. He joined the Labour party in 1931 and became a brilliant speaker. During the Second World War he was often critical of Churchill. In 1945 as Minister of Health in the Labour government he launched the National Health Service. Bevan wanted a very left-wing Labour party and quarrelled with other Labour leaders about this.

Bonham-Carter, Lady Violet (1887-1969) was Asquith's daughter and knew Churchill well. She married Sir Maurice Bonham-Carter in 1915 and all her life worked hard for the Liberal party. In 1965 she published a book, *Winston Churchill as I knew him,* which gives an interesting and sympathetic portrait of Churchill.

Boothby, Robert (1900-   ), now Lord Boothby, was a Conservative MP from 1924 to 1958. He was very independent in his views and supported Churchill over Munich. He knew Churchill well, was his Parliamentary Private Secretary 1926-29, and Parliamentary Secretary to the Ministry of Food 1940-41.

Chamberlain, Neville (1869-1940) was the son of Conservative politician Joseph Chamberlain and himself went into politics. He was Conservative Chancellor of the Exchequer 1923-24, chose the post of Minister of Health under Baldwin 1924-29 and from 1931-37 was again Chancellor of the Exchequer. As Prime Minister (1937-40), he was responsible for the negotiations with Hitler which led to the Munich agreement in 1938. His resignation in May 1940 was forced on him by his loss of Conservative support in the House of Commons. Chamberlain unselfishly agreed to serve under Churchill, until a serious illness overtook him later in the year.

Collins, Michael (1890-1922) was an Irish politician and leader of the Sinn Fein (the party working for Irish independence). He helped to negotiate the peace treaty with Britain in 1921 and was later killed by Irish extremists.

Curzon, Lord (1859-1925) was a Conservative politician. He was Viceroy of India

(1898-1905) and served as Foreign Secretary under Lloyd George (1919-22). In 1923 Curzon hoped to succeed Bonar Law as Conservative Prime Minister, but Baldwin was chosen instead. Curzon remained Foreign Secretary until 1924.

Davidson, J.C.C. (1889-1968) started his career as Private Secretary to the Conservative leader, Bonar Law (1915-20). He was a Conservative MP from 1920 to 1937 and for a time Chairman of the Conservative party (1926-30). He did not like Churchill.

de Gaulle, Charles, General (1890-1970) served with the French army in the First World War. In 1940, when France fell to the Germans, de Gaulle left for England to lead the "Free French". He defended French interests even against her allies and had many arguments with Churchill. In August 1944 he returned to liberated Paris to head the French government, but in January 1946 he retired. In 1958 he returned to political power and was President of the French Republic until April 1969.

Eden, Anthony (1897-1977) entered Parliament as a Conservative in 1923. He was Neville Chamberlain's Foreign Secretary (1935-38) but resigned after disagreements with the Prime Minister. In September 1939 he was made Dominions Secretary and from 1940 he was first Secretary for War and then Foreign Secretary in Churchill's government. He was very close to Churchill, and was regarded as the future leader of the Conservative party. After another four years as Foreign Secretary (1951-55) he at last succeeded Churchill as Prime Minister. In 1957 he resigned because of ill-health (and criticism of his handling of the Suez crisis in 1956). He was created Earl of Avon in 1961.

Eisenhower, David Dwight, General (1890-1969) was an American officer who served as Commander-in-Chief of the Allied armies in North Africa (1942-44). In 1944 he acted as Supreme Commander of the invasion of Europe. He and Churchill got on well, and when in 1952 Eisenhower was elected President of the United States Churchill visited him on several occasions. Eisenhower was re-elected at the end of his first term of office and remained President until 1961.

Fisher, Lord (1841-1920) was a British Admiral who was First Sea Lord 1904-10. Churchill insisted that he should be re-appointed in 1914, but Fisher was a difficult colleague, always threatening to resign. He actually did resign in 1915, over the Dardanelles campaign, and this helped to discredit Churchill.

Goebbels, Joseph (1897-1945) was a Nazi politician and Hitler's Minister of Propaganda. He committed suicide when Germany collapsed in 1945.

Halifax, Lord (1881-1959) was Chamberlain's Foreign Secretary at the time of Munich. In 1940 many Conservatives preferred Halifax to Churchill as Chamberlain's successor. However, as a member of the House of Lords, Halifax thought it would be difficult for him to be Prime Minister, and he stood down. Churchill sent him as ambassador to the United States (1941-46). He was created Earl of Halifax in 1944.

Hankey, Maurice (1877-1963) was Secretary to the Committee of Imperial Defence 1912-38, to the War Cabinet 1916-18 and to the Cabinet 1918-38. From 1940 to 1942 he served in Churchill's war-time government.

Hardie, James Keir (1856-1915), a Scottish miner, was one of the founders of the Labour party. He was MP for Merthyr Tydfil in South Wales from 1900 to 1915. In the House of Commons he spoke up boldly in support of workers and their causes. Hardie clashed with Churchill over the handling of the strikes

48 Keir Hardie, the Labour MP. He was fiercely critical of Churchill's handling of strikes and strikers in 1910 and 1911.

of 1910 and 1911. He was an experienced journalist and his articles and pamphlets were widely read.

Hitler, Adolf (1889-1945) was leader of the National Socialist German Workers' Party. He was made Chancellor of Germany in January 1933, silenced all opposition and ruled as Dictator. His determination to gain territory for Germany led to war with Britain and France in 1939. At home, Hitler established concentration camps for Jews and opponents of his government. When the Allies closed in on Berlin in April 1945, Hitler committed suicide.

Ismay, Hastings Lionel, General (1887-1965) was a British soldier who was Churchill's Chief of Staff from 1940 to the end of the war. His nickname was "Pug". In 1947 he was created Lord Ismay. From 1952 to 1957 he was Secretary-General to the North Atlantic Treaty Organisation (NATO).

Lloyd George, David (1863-1945) was a Welsh Liberal politician. He was a brilliant speaker and a supporter of social reform. He served as Chancellor of the Exchequer (1908-15) and Minister of Munitions (1915-16) and Secretary for War (1916) under Asquith, whom he replaced as Prime Minister in 1916. Lloyd George remained Prime Minister of a Coalition government until 1922. He stayed in the House of Commons and was Leader of the Liberal party 1926-31. At the very end of his life, in 1945, he accepted an earldom.

Macmillan, Harold (1894-   ) was, during the 1930s, one of a group of young, progressive Conservative MPs. Churchill made him Parliamentary Secretary to the Ministry of Supply in 1940 and later sent him as a special representative to North Africa. Although he lost his seat in the July 1945 election, he returned to the Commons at a by-election later that year. He was Minister of Housing (1951-54) in Churchill's last government and, after holding a series of high offices, became Prime Minister himself (1957-63). His autobiography tells us much about Churchill.

Montgomery, Bernard Law, General (1887-1976) was a British soldier, appointed commander of the Eighth Army in 1942. He won the battle of El Alamein (October 1942). In 1944 he commanded the British and American troops who landed in France on D Day. Montgomery had a strong personality and was sometimes difficult to work with, as the American Supreme Commander, General Eisenhower, found. In 1944 he was created Field Marshal and in 1946, Viscount Montgomery of Alamein.

Roosevelt, Franklin Delano (1884-1945) was President of the United States from 1932 to his death. He was eager for the USA to support Britain in 1940 by all means short of war. Churchill admired and liked him.

The two men exchanged many letters and met frequently during the war, which the Americans finally entered at the end of 1941.

Stalin, Joseph (1879-1953) became leader of Soviet Russia when Lenin died in 1924. He forced changes through with much bloodshed in the 1930s and eliminated opposition to himself. After the French and British failed to make an agreement with him to check German expansion, Stalin in August 1939 made a pact with Hitler. In 1941 he headed Russia's resistance to the German invasion, pressing Britain and later the USA to attack France to relieve pressure on Russia. At Tehran and Yalta, Stalin met and negotiated with Churchill and Roosevelt. In 1945, at the end of the war, Russian influence over most of central and Eastern Europe was supreme.

Wavell, Archibald Percival, General (1833-1950) was British Commander-in-Chief in the Middle East from 1939. He defeated the Italians in North Africa but lacked resources to fight successfully against the Germans there in 1941. Churchill, who did not appreciate or understand Wavell, removed him from his command in July 1941 and sent him to India instead. In 1943, Wavell was made Viceroy of India, where he remained until 1947. He was created Viscount in 1943 and Earl Wavell in 1947.

49 David Lloyd George was a close friend and colleague of Churchill in the early 1900s.

Glossary

Boers
Dutch settlers in South Africa. Before 1902, when they came under British control, their states, the Transvaal and Orange Free State, were independent.

Bolsheviks
Russian Communists who followed Lenin, the leader of the October 1917 Revolution in Russia.

by-election
An election to replace a member of parliament in a single constituency between general elections (e.g. if an existing MP dies).

Chanak crisis, 1922
The Asian shore of the Dardanelles was made a neutral zone in 1920 and Allied troops (including British soldiers under a British commander at Chanak) occupied the area. When the Turks under Mustapha Kemal were at war with Greece in 1922, they advanced towards the Dardanelles and threatened in September to take over Chanak. In the face of British determination to defend the area if the Turks attacked, Kemal finally gave way and on 10 October agreed to respect the neutral zone. Lloyd George's government was blamed by many British people for having been too quick to threaten the Turks with war — even though war had in the end been avoided. The Chanak affair helped to encourage the Conservatives to leave Lloyd George's Coalition government.

coalition government
A government made up of members of more than one political party.

confidence, vote of
A majority in the House of Commons in support of the Prime Minister and his government.

Congress
The parliament of the United States, consisting of two elected bodies, the Senate and the House of Representatives.

constituency
The district which a Member of Parliament represents.

Council of Europe
In August 1949 the Council of Europe was formed. Its aim was to encourage European unity, and its first members were Belgium, Denmark, Ireland, France, Italy, Luxemburg, the Netherlands, Norway, Sweden and the United Kingdom. There was a Committee of Ministers (from each member country) and a Consultative Assembly, to which members of each country's parliament were sent.

Churchill was one of the British MPs at the first meeting. He approved of some kind of European unity and had launched his United Europe Movement to support this idea in Britain. However, he was not sure how far Britain should go towards actually joining the kind of "United States of Europe" of which he had spoken in 1946. The Council of Europe, which had no authority over member states, was only the first step towards possible closer cooperation.

Dardanelles
The southern part of the Straits (strip of sea) connecting the Mediterranean and the Black Sea. The "Dardanelles campaign" of 1915 aimed at putting this sea-passage under British control.

dominion status
Self-government for an ex-colony which became an independent member of the British Commonwealth.

flying-bombs
German pilot-less 'planes loaded with high explosives and directed against Britain (London and the South East) in June, July and August 1944.

Free Trade
A system of world trade in which countries do not try to keep out foreign goods by putting high customs duties on them.

Führer
The German word for "leader". Hitler was called "Führer".

Gallipoli
The peninsula which forms the European shore of the Dardanelles and which Britain tried to take from the Turks in 1915.

General Strike
A strike by workers in key industries (e.g. railwaymen, dockers) in support of another group of workers (e.g. in 1926, the miners).

Gold Standard
This represented the value of a country's currency in gold. In 1925 Britain went "back on the Gold Standard" and set a fixed, high value on her currency (4.86 dollars to the pound). This made British exports very expensive.

Home Rule, Irish
Self-government for Ireland. The whole of Ireland was part of the United Kingdom until 1922.

IRA
The Irish Republican Army, which was determined to obtain independence for a united Ireland (North as well as South), by force if necessary. The IRA did not accept the Irish Treaty of 1921.

Irish Treaty, December 1921
Although in 1920 Northern Ireland (Ulster) accepted a new Irish Home Rule bill giving separate parliaments to North and South, the Irish Republicans in the South would not accept this arrangement. The IRA continued the fight against British rule. At first the British tried to put down the IRA by force, but in July 1921 a truce was made and a conference between the British and the Irish Republicans was agreed on. The Irish Treaty followed in December 1921. It gave Southern Ireland dominion status. Extremists in the South refused to accept the Treaty and civil war continued until 1923. However, the British government supported the new Irish government in Dublin in its fight against the extremists and in 1922 the Irish Free State (independent Southern Ireland) officially came into existence.

Munich Agreement
The agreement made on 30 September 1938 between France, Britain, Germany and Italy that Hitler should occupy part of

Czechoslovakia (the Sudetenland). The Czechs had to accept the decision.

National Government
A government with members from all political parties, set up at a time of crisis.

Parliament Act 1911
This restricted the power of the House of Lords, which in future could only delay, not completely reject, Bills already passed by the House of Commons. (A Bill has to go through both Houses of Parliament and be accepted by the Queen before it becomes an Act of Parliament.)

Pearl Harbour
An American naval base in Hawaii. On 7 December 1941 the Japanese launched a surprise air attack on the American fleet there, sinking five battleships. The incident brought the United States into the Second World War.

People's Budget
The name given to Lloyd George's budget of 1909 which increased death-duties and introduced supertax — higher income tax on those with large incomes. There was also to be a tax on profits from the sale of land. The rejection of this budget by the House of Lords led to a political struggle between the Liberal government and the Lords, and eventually to the reduction of the House of Lords' powers.

Second Front
The Russians, under great pressure from the German attack, wanted Britain and the USA to start a "second front" by invading Western Europe in 1942. Left-wing groups in Britain supported the idea, and slogans demanding "a Second Front now" were painted on walls. Churchill was determined that there should be no invasion until a really strong military force, with plenty of landing-craft to take it across the Channel, had been built up. He had

difficulty in convincing the Russians (and even some of the Americans) that delay was necessary.

Sudetenland
The Sudetenland, which was a border area of Czechoslovakia, was inhabited chiefly by Germans. From 1933 the Sudeten-German Party, which sympathized with the German Nazis, pressed for self-government for the Sudetenland. The Czech government granted this early in September 1938, but Hitler then decided to join the Sudetenland to Germany. His demands led to a crisis, as the Czechs refused to give way and called on their allies the French to help them. By the Munich Agreement of 29/30 September 1938, war was avoided; Britain, France, Italy and Germany agreed that the Sudetenland should be transferred to Germany, in spite of the wishes of the Czech government.

Tariff Reform
A plan put forward by the Conservative politician Joseph Chamberlain in 1903 to put customs duties on foreign imports. Chamberlain wanted to exempt goods from countries of the British Empire from these tariffs — an idea called "Imperial Preference".

TUC — Trades Union Congress
An association of British trade unions. Its elected General Council often negotiates with the government on behalf of its members.

Ulster
The name was originally given to nine Irish counties, but from 1920 applied to six of those counties, now "Northern Ireland". This area remained part of the United Kingdom and did not join the independent Irish Free State created in 1922. (The Protestant majority in the North did not want to unite with the Catholic South.)

War Council
In November 1914 the War Council replaced

the old Committee of Imperial Defence as the body in charge of military planning in Britain. Churchill, as First Lord of the Admiralty was a member. The War Council gave approval in 1915 to the Dardanelles expedition. In May that year, when Asquith reorganized his government as a coalition, the War Council was dissolved. In June a special Dardanelles Committee was set up, and when this in turn was dissolved in November 1915, a small War Committee took over the direction of the war. Lloyd George, Prime Minister from December 1916, altered the system yet again and used instead a War Cabinet of from 5 to 7 members.

White Russians
The supporters of the old Russian government against the Reds (the Bolsheviks) after the Russian Revolution in 1917.

Wilderness, political
When a politician quarrels with his party leaders, he "goes into the wilderness", that is, he spoils his chance of being given a government post.

Some Suggestions for Further Reading

For Younger Readers

Gilbert, Martin	*Winston Churchill*	OUP, Clarendon Biographies, 1966
Hoare, Robert	*World War One*	Macdonald, 1973
	World War Two	
	Winston Churchill	Cape
	(Jackdaw No. 31)	

For Older Readers

The *official biography*, begun by Randolph Churchill and continued by Martin Gilbert, is extremely interesting. It has additional volumes of source material (letters, memos, etc) which are fascinating to dip into. Churchill's own books (see Date List for titles), especially *My Early Life* and the six-volume history, *The Second World War,* also make good reading.

Good advanced studies of Churchill include:

Pelling, Henry	*Winston Churchill*	Macmillan, 1974 (Pan books, 1977)
Rhodes James, R.	*Churchill. A Study in Failure, 1900-1939*	
Taylor, Alan J.P. etc.	*Churchill: Four Faces and the Man*	Allen Lane, 1969

Places to visit

Chartwell Manor, near Westerham, Kent — Churchill's country house, now a museum containing many of his possessions.
The Imperial War Museum, London.

Index

Numbers in **bold type** refer to pages on which illustrations appear